D0047728

Things I Wish I'd Known Before I Started Sailing

Things I Wish I'd Known Before I Started Sailing

JOHN VIGOR

With a Foreword by Don Casey

Illustrations by Tom Payne

SHERIDAN HOUSE

First published 2005 by
Sheridan House Inc.
145 Palisade Street
Dobbs Ferry, NY 10522
www.sheridanhouse.com

Copyright © 2005 by John Vigor
Illustrations copyright © by John Vigor

All rights reserved. No part of this publication may be reproduced, stored in a retrieval system or transmitted in any form or by any means, electronic, mechanical, photocopying, recording, or otherwise, without the prior permission in writing of Sheridan House.

While all reasonable care has been taken in the publication of this book, the publisher takes no responsibility for the use of the methods or products described in the book.

Library of Congress Cataloging-in-Publication Data

Vigor, John.
    Things I wish I'd known before I started sailing / John Vigor ;
  with a foreword by Don Casey; illustrations by Tom Payne.
      p. cm.
  Includes bibliographical references and index.
  ISBN 1-57409-211-1
  1. Sailing-Handbooks, manuals, etc. I. Title.

GV811.V54 2005
797.124—dc22   2005011469

ISBN 1-57409-211-1

Printed in the United States of America

To Lindsay, Geoffrey, Devin, and Veronica

Contents

Acknowledgments

The basic material for this book comes from thousands of sources. They include fellow sailors, hundreds of books, thousands of magazine articles, and my own experience of thousands of miles of racing and cruising on lakes, rivers, reservoirs, and across oceans in many parts of the world.

It also comes from my being in the business of writing about people who sail and editing other people's writing about boating. Whether they know it or not, all these people have made contributions to my store of knowledge over a period of more than 40 years. I'm grateful to them even though I can't possibly thank all of them individually or even name them.

One person I should name, however, is the fine sailor who wrote the foreword to this book, Don Casey. It was with some trepidation that I approached Mr. Casey. He is, of course, a person of considerable stature among boating authors. My approach was necessarily oblique, since I didn't have an address for him. I e-mailed him on an Internet Website that invites readers to pose questions to him about boat maintenance and renovations. I fully expected the webmaster to discard my query as irrelevant but no, the miracle happened. It was forwarded to Mr. Casey. "Yes," he replied, "I'll do it for you. What's the deadline?"

Um, well, yes. I had to confess that I'd left this until the last moment. The publisher's deadline was three weeks away. And Mr. Casey was off cruising on his sailboat in the Caribbean with his wife, Olga. Somehow I had to e-mail the manuscript to him.

Suffice it to say he went to considerable trouble to receive the whole manuscript on his laptop computer in Martinique. I am humbled and grateful. There is indeed a brotherhood of the sea and Mr. Casey upholds its finest traditions.

Foreword

Let's be honest, shall we? Basic sailing requires about as much skill as, say, riding a bicycle. Borrow or rent a small sailboat and in a hilarious half hour of pulling strings and pushing on that stick thing, you will become skillful enough to be able to sail back to the dock with almost no risk of injury or serious property damage. All you will *wish you had known* before that initial outing is how easy it would be.

Well, let me not mislead; eventually you also may wish you had known how seductive sailing could be. Perhaps it is a sailboat's tactile connection to natural rhythms or its disconnect from land-based constraints, but for many sailing comes to hold far greater promise than an afternoon's diversion. We become enamored— some would say obsessed. When we should be concentrating on work, or listening to a spouse, or paying attention to the road, we are thinking about sailing. We are imagining more time on the water, scheming for a better boat, weighing our life choices.

Whether you wish to sail faster, to sail farther, or just to sail more confidently, the knowledge borne of experience is what you most need. But given the pace of sailing and the limited time most of us get to spend doing it, broad experience can be a long time coming. Thus most sailors just muddle along, improvising as necessary. I intended to say such improvisations can be unorthodox, but the truth is there is no orthodoxy where sailing in concerned. You need only ask the advice of two sailors on one issue to confirm this. That is where this book comes in.

My first introduction to John Vigor was nearly 15 years ago when *Cruising World* published the compelling account of his 1987 passage from South Africa to the United States. Five years later, our circles would intersect as we both wrote books for the same boat maintenance series. John's book, then named *The Sailor's Assistant* (since retitled *Boatowner's Handbook*), delivered more useful information in a small package than any boating book I had run across since the pocket-size *Royce's Sailing Illustrated.* It would become a well-thumbed reference, and I became a fan of John Vigor's economy with words.

John brings that economy to this book. He offers short-winded advice on nearly 200 subjects. A long career examining the sailing feats of others combined with more than half a century of personal sailing experience gives authority to John's take on each of these subjects. His invariably sound advice can either be adopted whole or used as a standard for evaluating alternatives. Either your technique or your confidence will get a boost.

Inexperienced sailors will surely find this book a fair current, carrying you forward at a significantly faster pace than you can muster on your own. For experienced sailors, it provides a strong breeze—perhaps fair, perhaps contrary—against which to test your skills. For sailors of all stripes, it is a downwind voyage under the command of a skillful captain. I, for one, am glad I signed on.

Don Casey
Le Marin, Martinique

Introduction

Whether you're new to sailing or have sailed all your life, there are always questions that need to be answered. But finding answers is never as easy as you might wish. It's often extraordinarily difficult to get good solid advice on some aspect or other of sailing. In a way, that's understandable because sailing is a sport that embraces dozens of wildly disparate disciplines—from advanced aerodynamics to boiling a pot of water during a storm—so it's not easy to find all the knowledge you need in one repository.

Ironically, however, what you'll frequently run into is not a lack of advice, but too much, especially from experienced sailors. They've all found their own ways of doing things on sailboats and the answers they'll give you are often simply too vague or too contradictory to make sense of.

If truth be told, many experienced sailors suffer from the nagging feeling that they're not doing things right. When he was in his seventies, the famous author E. B. White once confessed: "Lacking instruction, I invented ways of getting things done, and usually ended up by doing them in a rather queer fashion, and so did not learn to sail properly, and still cannot sail well, although I have been at it all my life." ("The Sea and the Wind that Blows," from *Essays of E. B. White*.)

I, too, have bumbled along through a long sailing career. I started sailing as a kid. I've raced and cruised across oceans. For years I was dogged by the suspicion that I was doing it all wrong, but I finally saw the light. I concluded that there are no absolutely right or wrong ways to do things on a sailboat. Whatever works at the time is the right thing. So what I offer here is advice about at least one way to do things right—methods that time and years of experience have proved successful.

There are undoubtedly many other ways of doing things right but if you follow the advice in this book you'll enjoy the confidence that comes from knowing you're not doing anything terribly wrong, that these things have been tried, tested, and found good by generations of sailors before you. This is a conservative book. It promotes a safe and simple philosophy toward sailing. It doesn't pretend to be all-inclusive or fully informative but it does provide sufficient information to reassure you and point you in the right direction for deeper research.

If this book has a goal, it is to encourage beginners of all ages to start sailing with confidence and to dispel some of those persistent myths prevalent among many experienced sailors. As a bonus, at the end of each entry you'll find a tip that should come in useful some day when you're afloat.

There are more than 180 subjects here, listed alphabetically, but you can open the book at any page and browse happily, creating a trail of your own by following the recommendations to see other related subjects.

The appendix contains a few tables and formulas I've found useful over the years, not only for practical reasons but also for testing the worth of advice offered by sailing friends and the truth of their claims about how fast their boats can sail. In addition, there's a list of books that would have been twice as valuable if I'd read them before I made all my own mistakes.

The talents of Tom Payne, a renowned artist and illustrator, have contributed greatly to the value of this book. You only have to glance at Tom's cartoons to know that he is a sailing man who has seen his fair share of incompetent skippers in his time.

In short, you have in your hands the book I wish I'd had when I started sailing. I am tempted to say that Mr. White should have had it, too; except that if he had, he wouldn't have been able to write so charmingly about not being able to sail properly.

Things I Wish I'd Known Before I Started Sailing

A

ADVICE

■ Good advice is very hard to find

Sailing a boat well requires an extensive knowledge of a surprisingly wide variety of skills and disciplines, ranging from cooking and navigating in rough water to the aerodynamics and hydrodynamics of a balanced hull and sails. So, all their lives, sailors are seeking answers to questions. And none more so than beginning sailors.

It can be very frustrating trying to get the information you need because the advice you receive from one sailor often conflicts with the advice from another. Unfortunately, what works for one sailor on one boat might not work for another on another boat.

Worse yet, the sailing world (and the Internet) is rife with half-truths propagated by people with little knowledge and less experience—and they're often the loudest with their advice.

So where do you find good advice? Why, here, of course. These are my recommendations:

1. Read books and magazines from reputable boating publishers. There are books on all subjects germane to sailing, and book publishers stake their reputations on checking and editing, so that the facts are correct.

2. Take lessons from instructors qualified by U.S. Sailing or the American Sailing Association.

TIP: Beginners should read *Sailing Fundamentals* by Gary Jobson.

ANCHORING

■ **There's more to anchoring than meets the eye**

We expect miracles of anchors, and mostly they oblige. But when you pause to consider the unknown nature of the invisible seabed, it must strike you that nothing could be less scientific than the act of lobbing overboard a lump of strangely shaped metal attached to a rope or a chain, and expecting it to hold your boat securely in place despite changing tides, swift currents, and strong winds. It smacks strongly of voodoo. Anchoring is thus more art than science.

Modern anchors are cleverly designed, but they still need weight to dig in. One pound of anchor weight per foot of boatlength is a good rule for plow anchors like the CQR, the most popular choice of long-distance voyagers. Fisherman anchors, good for rocky bottoms, need to be a couple of sizes heavier.

Boats of about 28 feet and up do well to carry all-chain rodes. If you're reasonably young and fit, you can raise a 35-pound anchor on $\frac{5}{16}$-inch chain from a depth of 90 feet without a winch. I've done it many times but it's easier if you can sit down and brace your feet.

TIP: A chain pawl on the bow roller is your best friend.

(See Windlass)

ASTERN GEAR

■ Some sailboats are impossible to steer in astern gear

When you put a full-keeled, heavy displacement sailboat into reverse, anything could happen. And it does. I've had more embarrassing experiences with astern gear under power than with anything else to do with boats.

Science tells us that a propeller revolving in a counter-clockwise direction as seen from astern will "walk" the stern to port. But on some boats, such as Carl Alberg's Cape Dories, which have keels cut away up forward, there's never any telling how fast they will walk. And if there's any decent wind blowing, they might even walk in the opposite direction until the hull is hanging downwind from the prop.

On some boats, when you touch astern gear, strange things happen. And never the same things twice. Other full-keelers like the Westsail 32 seem to be able to back up under perfect control, and fin-keel boats rarely have any problems.

So if you own one of these fractious vessels, you'd be wise not to rely on astern gear to slow you too much when you enter a slip.

TIP: You'd do well to learn how to back out into a narrow channel with the aid of a spring line to a cockpit cleat or winch.

(See Berthing)

AUTOPILOTS

■ Don't expect too much from an autopilot

Sailors soon discover that steering by hand for hours is boring, tiring, and irritating, especially when they're singlehanding. You can't even leave the tiller to make a cup of tea or plot a compass bearing unless you back the jib and heave to.

So the thought of handing over steering duty to an electronic helmsman who is happy to be on watch 24 hours of the day without pay, and who won't run off with your wife, is very attractive to sailboat owners.

Unfortunately, most autopilots, but particularly the affordable, cockpit-mounted pilots for tillers or wheels, are slow-witted and wimpish by nature. They are quite happy to steer when the sun is sparkling on calm water, but when it starts to blow they can't react fast enough. They get out of synch on big following swells and the boat wallows dangerously all over the place.

Keep the tiller pilot for calm weather under power.

TIP: When the wind starts to howl, you need a vane self-steering system such as an Aries, Monitor, or Windpilot. The vanes react instantly to wind changes and generate tremendous power from trailing oars. These are quick-witted helmsmen with muscles, right when you need them most.

AVOIDING COLLISIONS

■ **Despite all precautions, boats collide**

Sailboats collide with reefs, with ships, with containers washed off ships, and with timber logs. They collide with whales and they collide with each other.

The rules of the road cut down on collisions but they can't prevent all of them any more than automobile driving rules can.

To lessen the risk:

- Learn the Inland and International Rules for the Prevention of Collisions at Sea.
- Keep a good lookout at *all* times.
- Give way to big ships and vessels of any size that seem not to have noticed you, whether you have right of way or not.
- If in doubt, communicate. Use VHF radio on Channels 13

(bridge to-bridge) or 16. Use a signal mirror by day or a white flare at night to get noticed.

- Take a compass bearing at first sighting of a ship. If it changes, you'll stay clear. If it doesn't, make at least a 60-degree turn (to get noticed on radar) and speed out of the ship's path if possible.
- Keep a radar reflector permanently hoisted in your rigging.
- Carry a life raft or dinghy (with a handheld VHF radio) in which to abandon ship.

TIP: Install watertight bulkheads or foam flotation.

(See Radar; Right of way; Running lights)

B

BALANCED HELM

■ Bad hull and sail balance can be dangerous

Weather helm is an obvious sign of bad balance. It's very tiring to have to fight the helm just to keep a straight course.

Because the factors affecting hull balance are so changeable and complicated, good balance is extremely difficult to design deliberately, and a well-balanced boat often comes about by sheer chance.

According to the prominent naval architect J. Laurent Giles, good balance is "freedom from objectionable tendencies to gripe or fall off the wind regardless of angle of heel, speed, or direction of wind." A balanced boat, he maintained, should have "the utmost docility and sureness of maneuvering at sea, in good or bad weather."

World-renowned naval architect and research scientist C. A. Marchaj warns bluntly: "Seaworthiness cannot be achieved if the boat is badly balanced."

Hull balance may be upset when a boat heels and the underwater shape changes radically, lifting the stern and dropping the bows, for example. The tendency to gripe, or turn into the wind (which requires weather helm to counter it) is increased as a boat heels because the sails' driving force now comes from a point much farther out to one side.

TIP: Excessive beam carried well aft is a prime cause of bad hull balance.

(See Weather helm)

BASIC REQUIREMENTS

■ **What a cruising boat needs to go to sea**

Here, in order of importance, are the basic needs of an ocean-going cruising sailboat:

Seaworthiness
Comfort (seakindliness)
Self-steering
Speed

Seaworthiness is the ability of a boat to survive heavy weather without admitting much water down below or suffering severe damage to the rig. A seaworthy boat should be able to withstand a 180-degree capsize and recover quickly.

Comfort, or seakindliness, denotes a gentle motion at sea, often the result of a softly rounded, deep, heavy-displacement hull. But it's a comparative term. Few boats under 40 feet can be called seakindly, according to the eminent designer Howard I. Chapelle. The very design characteristics a small boat needs to survive bad weather make her react so jerkily that it's impossible to stand or walk without hanging on to something, he maintained.

A well-balanced hull will steer easily downwind under twin jibs with lines taken to the tiller, or at any angle to the wind if a mechanical wind-vane self-steering system is fitted. Such a system is the equivalent of a crewmember who never tires, complains, sleeps, or eats all the chocolate.

TIP: Speed, although last in this list, is still important in ocean voyaging for its effect on crew morale and the ability to avoid bad weather.

(See Simple solutions; Upgrading)

BATTENS

■ You don't need battens in your mainsail

No matter what the sailmakers and batten manufacturers tell you, it's not necessary to festoon your mainsail with battens. In fact, battens are a menace. The bigger they are, the worse the menace.

They hang up on the shrouds when you're trying to drop the mainsail. They get in the way when you're trying to flake the mainsail on the boom. Short battens wear through the sailcloth in front of the pocket with continual flexing. Full-length battens bear heavily against the mast and stress the leech, even if you spoil them with fancy, expensive batten cars.

Have you ever noticed that genoa jibs don't have battens? Why should a mainsail then? The only reason is to support a small curved area aft of a straight line from the mainsail clew to the masthead. It's a part of the mainsail that would just flop over if it weren't supported by battens. And it's the part that contributes most to weather helm, so it helps to get rid of it.

TIP: If you order a mainsail with a hollow leech like that on a genoa, you simply don't need battens. The small area of mainsail you sacrifice can be made up with a bigger jib.

BERTHING

■ **The hardest thing about sailing is parking the boat afterward**

I know deep-sea sailors whose greatest fear is docking the boat in a congested marina slip. They'd almost rather face a storm at sea than endure the ordeal of maneuvering at close quarters in a marina, especially a strange marina.

The basic trouble with berthing is that when you slow the boat down, she loses steerage way. That is, you lose control of her direction. Thus, if you approach your slip at a reasonable speed so you can steer, you're going too fast to stop the boat in her own length in the slip. But if you slow your approach for safety's sake, you simply can't steer.

It's no good pretending that practice makes perfect; the circumstances are never the same twice. There are always differences in the speed and direction of wind and current, and the number of idiots who get in the way as you line up your approach. You have to play it by ear every single time.

Heavy-displacement, full-keel sailboats are the hardest to control in close quarters, but the designers of marinas cut them no slack because they are in the minority.

TIP: Get fenders out well in advance, at least three each side.

(See Astern gear)

BILGE PUMPS

■ Don't rely on your bilge pump to save the boat

No matter how many mechanical pumps you have aboard, you still need at least two hand-operated bilge pumps. But even they won't cope with the inflow of water from a hole in the hull the size of a man's fist.

A normally fit crewmember would be lucky to pump 15 gallons of bilge water a minute for any length of time, and it doesn't take much of a hole to let in that amount. In fact, a hole only 1½ inches in diameter, located 6 inches below the waterline, will let in much more than that—about 21 gallons a minute.

So when the hull is badly cracked or holed, your first action should be to stop the boat and drag a sail or collision blanket over the hole from the outside. This will slow the inflow of water so your pumps can handle it while you figure out a way to tackle the problem from inside, by stuffing a pillow or mattress into the hole or making a more permanent repair.

TIP: The smaller the boat, the bigger the pump you need—but never underestimate the ability of a bucket to move large quantities of water in the hands of a frightened sailor.

BINOCULARS

■ Don't waste your money on high-powered binoculars

Be content with a modest magnification because the erratic motion of a small boat causes images to shimmer and blur in the eyepieces. The rule-of-thumb glasses for small boats are 7 x 50s. Anything more powerful is a waste of money.

Incidentally, 7 x 50 means the image is enlarged seven times, and the front lenses are 50 mm in diameter. The 7 x 35 format is quite popular, too, but the larger the front lens, the better the binoculars will gather light at night. The 7 x 50 format makes for good night glasses that will help you spot buoys and moored boats mostly invisible to the naked eye after sundown.

You can buy military spin-offs such as night scopes and image-stabilizing binoculars that provide steadier pictures and magnifications of as much as 14 times, but they will cost you an arm and a leg. They're heavy, full of vulnerable electronics, and they'll need a constant supply of batteries. Unless you're a professional spy, you really don't need them.

TIP: Good binoculars are expensive. Guard yours carefully and buy a second, cheap pair for visitors who keep changing your settings and dropping your glasses.

BOAT CATEGORIES

▪ **It's important to know what boats are designed for**

When it comes to choosing the right kind of boat for you, the first thing you have to realize is that boats that look a lot alike might be designed for quite different purposes.

Learn to recognize the give-away characteristics of boats intended for special kinds of sailing. For instance, a boat with a tiny cockpit, a deep fixed keel, and a bowsprit is almost certainly designed to cross oceans. A boat with a centerboard, a large open cockpit, and a mast in a tabernacle is probably intended for daysailing and trailering.

Boats are designed for all kinds of jobs from fishing to hosting cocktail parties, and it's vitally important that you find a boat that will do what you want it to. If you want to waterski behind your Westsail 32, you're going to be frustrated.

Sailboats fall into the following basic categories: daysailers; weekenders (which are daysailers with rudimentary overnight accommodation); coastal sailers; and deep-sea voyagers.

Voyagers are self-contained and able to stay at sea for weeks.

Coastal sailers are more lightly built, don't stray far offshore, and need ports of refuge every 30 to 50 miles.

TIP: Don't buy a coastal cruiser for an ocean passage unless you know how to upgrade it.

(See Boat choice; Boat design)

BOAT CHOICE

■ Decide on the kind of boat you need before you buy it

Ever noticed how many boats just sit in their marina slips on beautiful summer weekends? Too many of them are neglected because they're not what their owners need.

Boats are designed to be better at some things than others. If you buy a boat purely for racing, for example, it won't provide a comfortable weekend home for cruising.

A boat that's too big, too small, too slow, too ugly, too expensive to run or maintain, or not seaworthy enough will only lead to disappointment and disillusionment.

Before you buy, sit down and decide exactly what kind of sailing you want to do now and in the future. Figure out your initial expectations of a boat and how much you can afford to spend on it. Be very honest with yourself. This exercise will dramatically increase your odds of ending up with a boat that will meet your real needs.

Beware of love at first sight. It's true that looks are important, but try to concentrate initially on a boat's suitability for your practical needs.

TIP: Avoid excessively ugly boats because they indicate a serious lack of knowledge of design or construction. No useful boat need ever be ugly.

(See Boat categories; Boat design; Chartering; Prices)

BOAT DESIGN

■ Don't delude yourself—there is no perfect boat

No boat can be the best at everything. Boat design is a series of compromises. For speed you may have to sacrifice comfort or seaworthiness. For stability you may have to sacrifice accommodations, and so on. You simply can't have it all.

The hull, rig, and accommodations of a coastal cruiser are different from those of a dedicated ocean voyager, and so is performance. But within their categories boats don't differ greatly because they're the products of centuries of adaptation to seas and oceans whose habits haven't changed at all.

Most designers are conservative by nature but sometimes, at the behest of manufacturers' salesmen, they design aberrations such as coastal cruisers based on inherently unseaworthy designs for the International Offshore Rule.

Normally, however, any new design is a slightly changed old design. Even in these days of computer-assisted design, only about 1 percent is genuine inspiration. But that's enough, because an inch here and an inch there can make a telling difference in a boat's behavior.

TIP: You can learn to judge what a boat is best at simply by looking at it. Narrow deep hulls are tender but comfortable at sea. Beamy shallow hulls are stable and fast but not as seaworthy. Every boat tells its own story.

(See Boat categories; Boat choice)

BOAT DIMENSIONS

■ A few feet longer is a whole lot bigger

It comes as a surprise to beginners to learn how much a boat changes with a few feet of extra length. Comparing boat size is always difficult because of the laws of relatively and similitude. If you double the size of a boat all round you'll increase its volume (or displacement) by 8 times and its surface area by 4 times.

Even a modest increase from 36 feet to 42 feet can result in a boat that's surprisingly wider, deeper, heavier, more difficult to handle, and more expensive to buy and maintain. The design weight, or displacement, of a Catalina 36, for example, is about 13,500 pounds. But stretch the hull just another 6 feet (less than the length of one average bunk) and the Catalina 42 weighs in at 18,000 pounds. That's a whopping 33⅓ percent larger.

Another extraordinary result of increased length is increased stability. If you double the size of a boat, its stability increases by 16 times. That's why bigger boats can carry proportionately much more sail than smaller ones, and it's also why longer boats can be narrower than short ones.

TIP: Instead of asking yourself how big a boat you need, find out how small a boat you can get away with. You won't regret it.

(See Boat size)

BOAT SIZE

■ How big a cruising boat do you need?

No thoughtful sailor would want to go cruising or voyaging in a boat that's too big; but how do you know what's too small?

Here's a way to estimate the size of the boat you need. Take the total weight of the crew, food, and water in pounds and multiply it by 7.5. The result is the displacement of the boat you'll need, within 10 percent or so.

Estimate crew weight at 160 pounds each. Allow 15 pounds per person per day for food and water, plus a reasonable safety reserve.

For personal clothing and effects, add 5 pounds per person per day, with a maximum of about 100 pounds per person.

For example, a cruising couple on a 30-day ocean crossing would need the following: Food and water: 30 x 15 = 450 pounds, plus 10 percent reserves = 495 pounds. Clothing and personal gear: 200 pounds. Crew weight: 320 pounds. Total: 1,015 pounds. Times 7.5 = a boat of about 7,612 pounds displacement, or between 6, 850 and 8,374 pounds.

That adds up to a fairly heavy-displacement boat of 27 or 28 feet or a little longer boat of medium displacement.

TIP: Carl Alberg's famous 28-foot Pearson Triton fits neatly into the top end of this range.

(See Boat dimensions)

BOATYARDS

■ **Too many boatyards are expensive, untrustworthy, and incompetent**

The more you learn to work on your own boat, and the less you have to rely on professional boatyards, the happier and richer you'll be.

Boatyards are a great cause of unhappiness in the sailing world.

Compared with the automobile repair industry, boatyards are hardly regulated at all. But most boat owners are dependent on the services of boatyards because federal environmental restrictions dictate that boats shall be hauled out and repaired in areas where the harmful materials used may be contained, swept up, and removed.

Thus, boatyards have come to assume unreasonably large power over boat owners, and as history has shown, power has a habit of corrupting.

The Internet is rife with horror stories about boatyards: the crimes they commit and their exorbitant charges. But the boatyard is a devil you have to learn to deal with.

Before you have any repairs or maintenance done, make quite sure you and the yard understand where the job begins and ends. Never, ever, ask them to "fix anything else you notice while you're at it." Try to agree on a price before work starts, and arrange to be informed if they think they will exceed it.

TIP: Do your utmost to get everything in writing.

BOTTOM PAINT

■ Use great care when choosing an antifouling paint

Choosing a bottom paint is almost as complicated as choosing a wife or husband. If you make the wrong choice, the results are equally disastrous except that getting rid of the wrong paint involves a lot of physical labor as well as emotional pain.

Almost all antifouling paints now use powdered copper to discourage marine growth. Soft ablative or sloughing paints constantly wear away to expose new copper, leaving no solid build-up.

Harder, modified epoxy paints lose only the copper, not the paint. The copper particles gradually dissolve, creating tiny passages giving water access to more copper deeper in, until all the biocide is gone. You can scrub these hard paints to renew their potency but after a few years you'll face the big job of scraping off the thick and heavy layer of old, ineffective coats.

A new paint may react badly with the paint you had on before, and bubble and hiss like a witches' cauldron. Then the whole lot will have to come off immediately, right down to the bare wood or fiberglass. You may have to start all over with different sealers and primers and undercoats.

TIP: Obey the instructions on the can. Once you've found a paint that's compatible with your boat and your sailing waters, stick with it.

BROTHERHOOD OF SAIL

■ **Sailors always help other sailors**

Whether they realize it or not, sailors of all kinds belong to an ancient brotherhood. Sailors have never tamed the sea, never managed to make voyaging totally safe and predictable. So, instinctively, they recognize the need to rely on each other. Sailors the world over spontaneously help other sailors in need.

You'll find that the farther you stray from the highly developed countries, and the fewer your companion cruising boats, the greater will be the common bond that springs up among you and the tighter the circle of help.

When you need a tow through a narrow pass in a reef, or assistance with painting your boat's bottom on a tropical island, your fellow sailors will be there to aid you.

You will need to make your own deposits in this bank of goodwill, of course, by building up a reserve for the time when you need to make your own withdrawals.

Many lifelong friendships are formed among long-distance voyagers. Cruising often seems to consist overwhelmingly of saying goodbye to new acquaintances made on land but relationships between separating sailors inevitably remain close, and are often resumed with gusto at a later date.

TIP: Be generous with help, then it will be there when *you* need it.

BUILDING A BOAT

■ **Fools build boats for wise men to buy**

This sweeping statement was in vogue in the days before fiberglass, when many amateur boatbuilders underestimated the time, money, skill, and patience needed to build a seagoing boat. Often, their adventurous dreams died a slow death and they gave up before the boat was finished. Tired and disillusioned, they sold years of work and thousands of dollars in materials for next to nothing.

Nowadays, comparatively few adventurers build their own cruising boats because there is such a large supply of inexpensive old fiberglass boats that can be upgraded.

But it's still possible to fall into a similar trap. That's because it seems such a bargain to buy an old boat with a finished hull and decks. It seems that all you have to do then is replace the inside to your liking, install a new engine, and acquire a mast and some rigging.

Unfortunately, the hull and decks constitute only about one-third of the finished price of a sailboat. The accommodations, engine, and rig will cost at least twice that amount in cash and labor expended.

TIP: The best buy in cruising sailboats is often one that has just returned from a long voyage. It will have all the expensive cruising gear you need already in place and tested.

(*See Upgrading; Wooden boats*)

BULWARKS

■ **Low fences keep things on board**

One of the best friends a cruiser can have is a low fence around the outside perimeter of the deck. These fences to port and starboard are known as bulwarks. They stop all sorts of things sliding overboard when the boat is heeled—shackles, sails, lines, and human beings—and they're just as useful when your boat is at anchor or in port.

Compared with the fiddly little toerails of wood or aluminum provided on most modern boats, bulwarks impart a wonderful feeling of security, especially when you're fighting for a foothold as you make your way forward along the leeward deck.

Although only the most dedicated (and expensive) cruising boats have them these days, bulwarks are not difficult to add to most hulls, no matter what the material they're built from. I once owned a fiberglass 31 footer to which 4-inch wooden gunwales were added with complete success. Waist-high bulwarks would be preferable, of course, but impractical on smaller boats for obvious reasons. Bronze fittings are available, to which bulwarks can be fastened, or you can have them custom-made.

TIP: Bulwarks should be either raised half an inch or so above the deck level, or be provided with plenty of drainage ports to let green water drain off the decks quickly.

BUNKS

■ Never judge a boat by the number of bunks

Yacht sales and advertising staff love to describe a boat by the number of people it can sleep. There are 25 footers that can sleep six down below and two more in the cockpit under a boom tent. Beware. If you've ever tried to cruise under sail with seven others on a 25-footer you'll know that some boats have more bunks than is good for them.

If you're out for a weekend, you can sleep more people than you could on an ocean crossing because they'll be able to get out of each other's hair for a large part of the time by swimming overboard, exploring in the dinghy, or going ashore.

On a long voyage, however, serious tensions can arise from overcrowding. Boats up to about 35 feet don't need more than four bunks, and smaller boats dedicated to ocean cruising are often handled by couples, in which case only two berths are needed.

Incidentally, a proper berth should be 6 feet 2 inches to 6 feet 6 inches long and 21 to 28 inches wide. One berth in four may be only 6 feet 1 inch long.

TIP: Some modern production boats squeeze in bunks that are too short. Test them before you buy.

C

CAPSIZE

■ Most boats are capsized by waves, not wind

Any voyaging sailboat may be turned upside down by a breaking wave with a height equal to (or greater than) 55 percent of the boat's length. That's the conclusion of tests performed at Southampton University, England. Thus, a 20-foot breaker could turn a 35-foot sailboat through 180 degrees.

Are there many 20-foot waves out there? Yes, plenty. But luckily you won't find many that big if you follow the established trade-wind routes and time your passages correctly.

But it's always possible. Extra-large waves do occur with sufficient frequency that they should no longer be referred to as "freak." Separate wave trains ride on each other's backs, and when three or more coincide, a very large wave may result.

European Space Agency satellites scanning the world's oceans for just three weeks in 2001 identified at least 10 individual waves at least 25 meters (81 feet) high. That was more giant waves than the scientists had anticipated.

You can expect 20-footers to be much more common. In fact, a wind of 40 knots blowing for 40 hours on open water can generate 20-foot waves.

TIP: If you're planning to cross an ocean, make sure your boat is watertight and will recover quickly from a total capsize.

(See Freak waves; Stability; Stability, tenderness)

CARBON MONOXIDE

■ Be very aware that these fumes can kill you

Almost every boat afloat generates carbon monoxide at some time or other, and this gas is a killer. It's invisible and it doesn't smell, but it's fatal in big enough doses.

Carbon monoxide is created whenever combustion takes place. It's a by-product of kerosene and propane burners in lamps or galley stoves. It's formed in unvented cabin heaters and it's present in exhaust gases from gasoline and diesel engines that are sucked over the transom into the cockpit and cabin. Charcoal barbecue grills are particularly potent sources of the lethal gas.

There are two important things you need to know about carbon monoxide:

- It has such a great affinity for human blood that it prevents oxygen from being transported to your body cells; and
- It can travel "upstream" against a fast-moving body of air.

A heavy concentration of the gas can kill you in minutes. Usually however, the process is slow and insidious. The symptoms start off with dizziness, headache, torpor, nausea, and uncon-sciousness, after which death follows swiftly.

If carbon monoxide is being generated, you need a plentiful supply of fresh air down below, no matter how cold the weather.

TIP: Install a battery-operated carbon monoxide alarm in every sleeping area.

CHARTERING

■ A quick way to find the type of boat you need

If you want to enjoy sailing, it's vitally important to find exactly the right boat. But that's easier said than done, especially for a newcomer to the sport. It can be daunting to walk around a crowded marina and see all the different kinds of boats. How can you tell if one is right for you? It's not like buying a car, where you can ask for a test drive. Or is it?

Perhaps there is a way.

If you have whittled down your prospective boat's list of desir-able features, why not find a charter company that rents out that kind of boat? A weekend of sailing on her, or even a day, would tell you just about all you need to know—that is, whether you could fall in love with her or not.

Most of us would find it too expensive to charter extensively but if you've done your homework you'll know whether you want a full-keel ketch or a fin-keel sloop, so you can reduce the field drastically.

TIP: The commonest caveat about buying a boat is: Never buy with-out a survey. Don't rue the cost. The same precept applies to charter-ing before you buy. The money spent will save you much more.

(See Boat choice)

CLEATS

■ Most cleats are far too small

Boatbuilders are notoriously mean with the size of cleats they supply. Perhaps they have daintier fingers than common sailors or use thinner lines but I think it far more likely that it's the bottom line that makes their decision for them.

They fear the wrath of the firm's ferocious financial manager much more than the complaints of a wimpy bunch of sailors, so they inevitably install smaller, cheaper cleats that simply won't accept a decent couple of turns of a jib sheet or main halyard with a locking turn on top.

Now we shouldn't have to put up with this. There are enough frustrations on small sailboats without our having to wrestle with piddling, undersized cleats on a bucking, heeling deck.

Throw the little monsters out. Give them to your dinghy-racing friends. Replace them with sailor-sized cleats and bolt them firmly in place.

The length of a proper cleat is 16 times the diameter of the line used with it. That means nothing less than a 6-inch cleat for ⅜-inch line, or an 8-inch cleat for a half-inch anchor line.

TIP: Fasten a cleat so that it's angled about 15 degrees across the line of pull, then the line won't jam on itself.

CLIMBING THE MAST

■ Never trust anyone who hauls you up the mast

Most sailboat masts are high enough that falling from one could kill you. So never hand over the responsibility for your safety when you go up the mast. It's your life and your responsibility.

If you're using a bosun's chair make sure it fits, so you won't fall out backwards. Always presume that the person winching you up will accidentally let go the halyard at some stage, or the winch will fail.

Tie a spare halyard under your armpits and have a second reliable crewmember take the slack out as you ascend. Make sure both halyards are firmly cleated while you're working aloft, and use a personal safety tether if there's something up there to fasten it to. Seriously, you can't be too cautious.

Prepare a safety tether and a halyard if you're using a rock-climbing ascender, mast steps, or one of those luff-groove ladders. Don't underestimate how much the mast jerks sideways when someone moves on deck below and how easily you can lose your footing.

TIP: Don't trust metal shackles. Use a bowline to attach the halyard to your chair.

COAST GUARD POWERS

■ You can't stop the Coast Guard boarding you

For many years the U.S. Coast Guard has enforced Congress's draconian laws that authorize the boarding and searching of private boats anywhere at any time without search warrants.

No good reason has ever been advanced to explain this heavy-handed discrimination against a small section of American citizens. You sometimes hear the excuse that it's part of the effort to keep illegal drugs from reaching the States, but nobody explains why law-enforcement agencies can search boats without probable cause, but not cars or houses.

The Coast Guard, long ambivalent about whether it is part of the military or of law enforcement, now is part of the federal Department of Homeland Security and seems to have tilted more toward the former. Thus—and certainly while the wide-ranging provisions of the U.S.A. Patriot Act are in effect—boat owners can expect to be targeted and boarded more frequently than ever before.

TIP: You don't have to *agree* to being boarded—but they don't need your permission, either. You can't prevent an armed party from boarding your boat. All you can do is follow the example of that legendary Victorian actress who was so wickedly used by the depraved bishop: Just shut your eyes and think of England.

COCKPITS

■ Too many cockpits look waterproof but aren't

No boat can be called properly seaworthy if her cockpit isn't totally waterproof. You might not consider this necessary if you habitually sail in calm waters, or even if you are a coastal cruiser but never stray far from land. But beware: if your cockpit ever *does* fill up with water from a rogue wave, an astonishing amount will find its way below, especially if you lack a proper bridge deck.

Most cockpit locker lids on production boats have deep gutters to shed rain and spray. They look very sleek and nautical but in fact they aren't watertight. They don't lock down tight against a seal. Don't trust them.

In the case of a 180-degree capsize, many heavy locker lids would also fall open. Enough water would flood the bilges to sink a boat in minutes. Even on a daysailer, you need to dog down the locker lids with secure hasps.

Most boats also have other holes in the cockpit area for engine instrument panels, gear levers, bilge pumps, and sundry equipment. Many of these holes will admit water under pressure and sometimes in copious quantities.

TIP: Use a garden hose to find the leaky spots in your cockpit, and fix them.

COMMON SENSE

■ It's your best ally—but do you have it?

When you start handling a boat they tell you it's all a matter of common sense. And yes, I have to admit that common sense is very useful on a sailboat, but it has to be the right *kind* of common sense.

What is common sense, exactly? The dictionary says it's sound practical judgment. I'd define it as the knowledge and experience an average person might reasonably be expected to have gained in the course of an ordinary life. And there's the flaw. There's no such thing as an average person or an ordinary life.

So if your common sense is of the variety that gives you an instinctive feel for mechanical things, the laws of physics, and the ways of wind and wave, count yourself lucky.

If, however, you're loaded with common sense about family relationships, infant nutrition, and crocheted afghans, you'll find those admirable traits not overly useful on a boat.

Common sense is supposed to help us in emergencies, of which there is an infinite variety on a boat, but I don't believe it's reasonable to expect anyone to have common sense for *all* of them.

TIP: Experience is what counts most. The more you sail, the less you need rely on common sense.

COMPASSES

■ Most magnetic compasses don't point to magnetic north

Boy Scouts tell you your compass points to magnetic north. When you start sailing a boat, you find out they're lying. Boat compasses don't point to magnetic north, or true north. In fact, there's hardly any telling where a boat compass might be pointing.

The trouble is deviation. Boy Scouts don't have deviation but boats do. They have engines, electronic instruments, and lumps of metal that attract the magnetic compass and cause it to deviate from magnetic north.

That wouldn't be so bad if the amount of deviation were consistent, but it isn't. Deviation changes with the heading of the boat. That makes the correction of deviation complicated. It involves swinging the compass and drawing up a deviation table for every course you could possibly sail.

Luckily, the maximum amount of deviation is usually small, say 5 degrees or so. That fact, combined with the bother of correcting it, makes most amateur sailors ignore deviation and set it to one side for attention later, as one does with a smelly old uncle at a family reunion.

TIP: If you're on a long trip, do the correction for deviation. If you're out by only 5 degrees, you'll be a whole mile off course for every 11.5 miles run.

COMPROMISES

▪ Every boat has disappointments

Newcomers to boats are inevitably blinded by passion. The visceral excitement of owning a beautiful boat makes them overlook obvious faults. But weeks later, after the honeymoon, they start to notice the shortcomings. She's slow. She has weather helm. The toilet smells. The stern gland leaks.

Some of these things you can change; some you can't. You have to realize that every boat has its imperfections and every seller tries to hide them, but basically you have to accept boats as they are, warts and all. None is ever perfect. All are compromises.

Practically, there are things you can do. Take deep breaths. Recite your boat's good points. Pretend she's your human partner and thank your lucky stars she will never run off to Rio de Janeiro with your neighbor and your bank account. She will never have an affair with another boat. She will never crash your car or serve you indigestible lasagna. She may max out your credit card with a bit of cosmetic surgery from time to time, but she will never vote for the politician you hate most or demand to be taken to the opera.

Isn't that compensation enough?

TIP: As a buyer, the lower your expectations, the fewer your disappointments.

COOKING AT SEA

■ The hardest part of ocean sailing is cooking

Cruising stories often make heroes of deck crews who brave howling winds and fearsome waves to navigate a small sailboat across an ocean. Very rarely do they give credit to the real hero, the cook.

Galley space is very limited on a small boat, and the galley tilts and lurches so violently that in heavy weather it's impossible to do more than boil water or heat a can of soup.

You have to plan your cooking step by tedious step. You can't just set a dish down on the counter. It will be flung off immediately. You can't even perform a simple act such as pouring from a kettle into a mug until you know the trick, which is to hold one in each hand and pour fore-and-aft, never athwartships.

The fiddles and potholders are never high enough, the galley stores are always buried way up forward, and at the end of it all the crew . . . well, the no-good crew will either spurn your meal because they're seasick or complain that you never, ever give them enough.

The cooks are the ones who deserve the medals.

TIP: Never pick up a hot pan until you know where you're going to put it down.

COOKING WITH ALCOHOL

■ **Here's a slow, expensive way to cook**

In the 1960s and early '70s, cooking on boats was often done with kerosene stoves. To start off, you had to pre-heat the stove with flaming alcohol in a cup around the burner.

All too often, however, people would turn on the burner too soon. The result would be a frightening flare-up of heated, but not vaporized, kerosene. Scorched galley curtains were common on boats of that era, while beards and eyebrows were rare.

The serious risk of fire forced boatbuilders to convert to pressurized alcohol stoves, on the premise that you can put out an alcohol fire with water. Many boats afloat today still have them, despite the fact that denatured alcohol is horribly expensive and burns much cooler than kerosene.

But you also have to pre-heat alcohol pressure stoves, so flare-ups continued until the modern *non-pressurized* alcohol stove came along. It's the nautical equivalent of a large expensive candle.

Liquid petroleum gas is more economical and convenient to cook with, but it sometimes sinks into bilges and explodes, so those who are afraid of it are doomed forever to the frustration of alcohol cookers.

TIP: If you have a pressure burner, fill the alcohol cup with fiberglass cord sold for woodstove gasketing, then the alcohol won't spill.

CREW OVERBOARD

■ **If you go overboard at night, say goodbye**

George Day, a past editor of *Cruising World* magazine, wrote this in his book *Safety at Sea*: "There is a strong correlation between losing sight of a victim and the fatality of that victim." In other words, if you fall overboard and the crew can't see you, they can't rescue you.

At sea in anything except a dead calm, your chances of being saved at night are very bleak indeed. In fact, if you don't have a light with you, they're about zero. Even if you're wearing one of those personal strobe lights that attach to your arm, your chances aren't a whole lot better.

An electronic flash may look quite bright, but when it's so low down on the surface of the water its range is very limited. At five knots, a boat travels about 10,000 yards in 60 minutes. She therefore covers 100 yards in 36 seconds, so by the time the first minute has elapsed the victim is nearly 200 yards away. Given the usual conditions of swells, breaking waves, and spray, that's too far.

TIP: The message is clear. Take extra precautions to stay aboard at night. Wear a harness and make sure there are strong attachment points in the cockpit and on deck.

(See Safety harnesses)

CREW PROBLEMS

■ You may have to singlehand more than you thought

Too many boats rot in port for want of a crew. Neophyte sailors soon discover that finding and keeping a regular crew is difficult. Human beings are hard to organize and often seem to have strange priorities. It's amazing how often otherwise reasonable crewmembers will decline to come for a sail because they'd rather take their spouses out for an anniversary lunch, or watch their kids perform in some silly play at school. So, if you don't want your boat to rot in port, be prepared to sail singlehanded.

But here's the question: If you have a boat that you usually sail with three others, is it too big for you to handle alone? To a large extent, the answer depends on your strength and experience, but the old rule of thumb said that there were two main limiting factors:

1. Can you raise and stow the heaviest anchor?
2. Can you reef and furl the largest sail?

If you feel confident that you can do both those things without help, singlehanding is probably within your capability.

TIP: Electronic autopilots, roller reefing, electric windlasses, and bow thrusters make it possible to handle a larger boat than you could otherwise manage—as long as all the gear works.

CRUISING BLISS

■ **There's no greater bliss than a perfect sailing day**

For as long as I can remember, I've had a recurring dream. There is never much detail, just a cruising sailboat, about 30 feet in length, coming in from the sea to a sheltered anchorage. It's almost dark. The friendly light of an oil lamp glows in the portholes. A man, the only person aboard, lowers the anchor over the bow. That's all.

I guess there's no explaining why I keep having this dream. A psychiatrist might be able to tell me what it really means, but I'm not sure I'd want to know. My mind is made up already: It's the end of a perfect sailing day.

For me, that's a gentle day, with the wind somewhere between 10 and 15 knots and all sail set on a broad reach. Wavelets sparkle in warm sunshine and the bow wave hisses quietly, sending white clouds of frothy bubbles tumbling aft past the cockpit. The current flows with me, of course. My destination lies in plain sight, and no rocks or reefs block my passage.

Ah, nirvana. What utter bliss. It's a strangely spiritual experience in a highly materialistic world, but a feeling all sailors will understand.

TIP: The more you sail, the greater your chances of a perfect day.

CRUISING COSTS

■ **Cruising can empty your bank account**

Someone in San Francisco once asked the renowned French deep-sea cruiser Bernard Moitessier how much it costs to go cruising permanently. "Just as much as you have," Moitessier replied.

He was right. It seems to be one of the unwritten laws of cruising that your cruising expenses follow the pattern of your every-day spending ashore, and for most of us it means that what we have, we spend.

In these days of easy credit, however, it's possible to spend a whole lot more than you have. That's a trap. You can waste years of prime cruising time working at home to pay off a fancy yacht.

It's far better to temper your spending to your shorn bank account. Make do with a smaller, more rudimentary boat if you have to, and cruise within your means. The lure of a bigger boat is always hard to resist, but if you can manage it, your cruising life will reward you with great dividends in the form of less boat mainte-nance, greater independence, fewer financial strains, and more sightseeing ashore.

TIP: Many couples have sailed around the world in boats of 30 feet or less, among them Lin and Larry Pardey. They built their en-gineless wooden cutter *Taleisin* themselves.

CRUISING DREAMS

■ **Most dreams of cruising never come true**

Many people dream of cutting and running. They dream of sailing into the sunset on a small boat of their own. They dream of blinding white tropical beaches and waving palms, of moonlit nights at an-chor in exotic lagoons, and lazy days of sunshine with balmy winds. It's a wonderful dream, but few people manage to make it come true.

After 14 years of world cruising in their own boat, Lin and Larry Pardey concluded that the success rate for would-be circumnavigators is between 10 and 20 percent. The Pardeys, perhaps North America's most famous cruising couple, figure the success rate for people who plan a cruise lasting between six and 18 months is 35 to 45 percent. Of the rest (55 percent to 65 percent of those who harbored plans), many don't manage to get away at all, or abandon their voyages along the way.

Surprisingly, it's not usually money or seasickness that's the problem. More often it's human incompatibility. Living space is extremely restricted on a boat and tempers flare easily among crews in such confined quarters. Life afloat requires special relationship skills.

TIP: Many of the most successful cruises are made by couples in modestly sized boats they can handle themselves without crews.

CURRENTS

■ **There's invisible danger in currents**

Good navigators have what amounts to a sixth sense for horizontal movement. Once you realize that the water you're moving through is itself moving; once you can visualize the course of your boat resulting from both its movement and the current's movement, you're well on the way to becoming a good navigator.

Currents are dangerous because they set boats off course. The result is that you're not actually going where you appear to be going.

Because currents are invisible, the only way you can ascertain their set and drift (direction and speed) is by taking bearings for fixes, and comparing the course and distance you've steered with the course you've covered over the ground.

This is usually easier to do in pilotage, with land visible, than at sea, where you need celestial navigation. Your GPS will do these calculations for you, of course, and tell you how far you've drifted off your rhumb line, but it's important that you should have an understanding of the principles involved and a true navigator's gut feeling for the way to correct for current.

TIP: In 12 hours, a wind blowing in a steady direction will create a surface current moving at about 2 percent of average windspeed.

(See Tides)

D

DANGER

■ The sea's not as dangerous as you might think

Most of the famous singlehanded circumnavigators of the mid-20th century sailed without lifelines around the deck, and without safety tethers.

For many, lifelines represented false security. "Better learn to cling like a monkey," Bernard Moitessier once told me. He has a point. I suspect that if I fell from atop the house of my 27-foot sloop while she was well heeled, I would fall right *over* my lifelines without touching.

It's impossible to know if lifelines have added to safety at sea on small boats but I don't think anyone can seriously say the death rate in the old days was any greater than it is now. And it's now one of the safest sports. More people die in their baths every year.

Perhaps the sea just *seems* more dangerous because we live in a society obsessed with safety, our own and others. We are ordered to belt up in cars, wear helmets on bicycles, put on sunscreen, and swallow vitamins. Old-timers accepted responsibility for their own safety and relied on common sense rather than constant and irritating adjurations from so-called authorities.

TIP: Never clip a safety tether on lifelines. They're not strong enough. Make fast to the base of a stanchion if necessary.

DINGHIES

■ **The dinghy of your dreams is no more than that**

One of the hardest decisions a cruising sailor faces is what kind of dinghy to choose. In many ports and anchorages, you need a dinghy to get ashore. A "hard" dinghy of wood or fiberglass is preferable to an inflatable. It's cheaper, longer lasting, drier, more seaworthy, easier to row, and more economical to run. But the smallest hard tender for a couple is about 7 feet long, and few small cruising yachts can find space on deck for it.

So most sailboats under 35 feet have to choose inflatables. They're prone to damage from the sun and from being scraped over rocks and pebbly beaches. They row so badly that they need outboard motors, and even when it's deflated a small one will take up a whole berth in the forepeak. Inflatables are comparatively expensive and very attractive to thieves.

Long-term voyagers, who treat them roughly, replace their inflatables every three or four years. A hard dinghy, easily maintained and repaired by its owner, has an almost indefinite lifespan.

TIP: Hard, nesting dinghies take up less space. But you need room to bolt them together before launching. It can be a riot trying to join two separate pieces on the waters of a choppy anchorage.

(See Tenders)

DIRECTION-FINDING RADIO

■ **If you know where the music's coming from, you can find your way home in fog**

In the days before loran and GPS, sailors used a crude but useful navigation system called radio direction finding (RDF). It was based on the fact that a ferrite-rod antenna on a simple AM radio receiver will show a distinct drop in signal strength when the antenna is pointed end-on toward the broadcasting station.

This silent, or near-silent spot was known as the null, and when it was combined with a magnetic compass you could take a rough bearing of the broadcast station. Two or more radio stations would give you an approximate position fix in darkness, rain, and thick fog. That was a very valuable aid in the days before satellite navigation and it's one you can still make use of in an emergency.

Some large-scale charts show the locations of AM broadcast stations, so all you have to do is swing your ordinary portable radio around the horizon until you find the null. Then you can home in on the station in any kind of weather, but with this caveat: you must be perfectly sure you know where the transmission is coming from.

TIP: Cheap radios give the best results. Expensive ones deliberately don't provide a very distinct null.

(See Navigation aids)

DISMASTING

■ **Losing a mast is not the end of the world**

Few yachts lose their masts at sea. When it happens, it's usually because of a rollover, a 180° capsize. It's serious, of course, but it's not the end of the world.

It always astonishes me that more masts don't go overboard, considering their narrow support base. Ocean-going sailors were suspicious for many years of the tall masts needed for Bermuda rigs. Shorter, more rugged masts on gaff-rigged yachts could be stayed more efficiently and were far less likely to be lost in a capsize.

Modern masts do fall down from time to time but crews inevitably bring their boats home under jury rigs concocted from the spars they can salvage and sails trimmed to fit. A keel-stepped mast most often breaks several feet above deck, so there's a handy stump left to work with. A deck-stepped mast might even be recovered whole, but raising it at sea can prove impossible, so makeshift jury rigs usually use booms, spinnaker poles, boathooks and other odds and ends to make a mast one-third to one-half the height of the old one. Sails such as jibs are usually set sideways and are surprisingly efficient.

TIP: Always carry a pair of heavy-duty wire cutters and plenty of wire clamps.

DISPLACEMENT

■ Never trust a broker's estimate of displacement

The displacement of a boat gives you a better idea of her size down below than does her overall length. A heavy-displacement cruising 30-footer, for example, may have almost twice the displacement of her lightweight racing sister, and therefore twice the accommodations.

But for some reason, heavy displacement has become a dirty word among boat dealers and brokers. Boats sell better these days if they are light and beamy. So when a broker talks about displacement, it usually isn't the true displacement at all.

The real displacement of a boat, as calculated by her designer, is the weight of the hull, deck, mast, sails, rigging, ballast keel, accommodations, fuel and water tanks at least half full, food, normal crew, and all other equipment on board. This can be 25 percent to 50 percent greater than the broker's figure, which is usually based on the weight of the hull, deck, accommodations, and rig only.

This bias against heavy displacement in sailboats is misplaced. Heavy boats are just as fast as light boats when the ratio of sail area to displacement is equal. Heavy boats can accept greater loads and are far more comfortable at sea.

TIP: If you're buying a boat, ask if her displacement figure includes the crew, stores, water, fuel, etc.

DOCUMENTATION

■ Your boat is a little piece of your country

If you're planning to sail to a foreign country you need a passport. Your boat needs one, too, and the best kind is a documentation certificate from the U.S. Coast Guard.

A U.S.-documented boat has privileges. Under international law, she is a piece of the United States, and therefore not to be trifled with. Documentation affords her the protection of U.S. consular officials anywhere in the world. She also earns the right to fly the special Yacht Ensign in home waters.

Federal documentation legally establishes her ownership and her nationality beyond a doubt. It's true that U.S. vessels with nothing more than state registrations have sailed around the world, but the recognized and accepted standard (when a boat is big enough) is documentation. State registration is not legal proof of nationality even though it's accepted for convenience in America's neighboring countries.

The minimum volume for documentation is 5 tons net, and for practical purposes in this case the Coast Guard measures net tons as ‰ of gross tons. That translates to a heavy-displacement vessel of about 25 feet or a moderate-displacement craft of about 30 feet in length.

TIP: A documented vessel is safer to buy, because her certificate must reflect all liens, mortgages, and liabilities against her.

DOWNWIND SAILING

■ Tacking downwind is sometimes very smart

Until you've tried it, you'd think that running dead before the wind is the easiest and most efficient course for a sailboat to steer. But the Bermuda rig now found on almost all small cruising sail-boats is biased toward upwind performance. On downwind legs, it suffers from some serious deficiencies.

For example, when the mainsail is eased out at right angles to the wind, the belly of the sail bears against the shrouds, where it constantly chafes. It also blankets the headsail. If you decide to run wing-and-wing, with the mainsail on one side and the headsail on the other, you have to extend the foot of the headsail with a long pole attached to the mast, and you must steer a hair-raisingly exact course to avoid accidentally jibing the mainsail.

A better idea in light weather is to tack downwind, so that the jib just fills. About 20 degrees off the wind should do it, and that adds only 6 percent to the distance covered. If the power of the jib adds 6 percent or more to your speed in light weather, you'll get there faster.

TIP: In heavy weather it doesn't pay to tack downwind because the boat is already moving at its fastest.

(See Trade winds)

DRINKING SEAWATER

■ **Yes, you can drink seawater, but ...**

Many of the old-time cruising heroes used to drink seawater regularly. Captain John Voss drank a glass a day for his health, and Sir Francis Chichester said an occasional drink of salt water helped relieve the leg cramps he suffered from, presumably caused by excessive sweating in the tropics.

So no matter what people say, you *can* drink seawater. But there is a catch: you must drink plenty of fresh water as well. Doctors say that seawater alone is about as harmful as no water at all.

In an emergency, you can get sufficient moisture to keep yourself alive from fish and plankton. Dr. Alain Bombard, a French physician, proved that in 1952 when he crossed the Atlantic in a rubber boat. He carried no water, but lived on fish, plus plankton he caught in a fine-mesh net he dragged astern at night. He wasn't in the best shape after his crossing, but at least he demonstrated that castaways without provisions need never give up hope.

TIP: Prolonged seasickness can seriously upset the balance of fluids in your body, so drink half a cup of seawater a day. You probably won't keep it down long, but your tissues will quickly absorb the vital minerals they need.

(See Freshwater supplies; Plankton; Water)

DROWNING

■ **You can drown as easily near the shore as at sea**

Beware of the false feeling of safety you get when you're close to land. Most water-related deaths occur near land, not out at sea. Be particularly careful in a hard dinghy. If it founders or capsizes you might never make it to shore.

Inflatable dinghies are less likely than hard dinghies to capsize, but they are more likely to be blown out to sea if the engine fails.

Most of us suffer from the delusion that if we can see the shore, we can swim to it. But that doesn't take into account the effect of the current or the coldness of the water. In areas where the water is cold, you'd be lucky to survive for an hour before hypothermia set in.

The biggest danger lies in overloading a hard dinghy. Choppy waves may flood the boat and lead to capsize. So check the dinghy's safe carrying capacity label. If there's no label, multiply overall length by beam in feet, and divide by 15, to find the maximum number of persons.

TIP: Make up a small safety pack for your dinghy (besides oars and lifejackets): flashlight, compass, bailer, and spare drain plug. A hand-held VHF radio could be a lifesaver.

E

ELECTROLYSIS

▪ **This corrosion is one of boating's great mysteries**

Strange things happen on a boat when one kind of metal touches another. Even two different kinds of metal some distance apart will react if they're in seawater and joined by a wire. They form an electric cell, and one metal starts to eat away the other. The effect is severe and can be rapid. There is still a lot of mystery attached to it.

It's commonly known as electrolysis, though the correct term is galvanic corrosion. Metals close to each other on the galvanic scale have little effect on each other, but those at either end can react strongly. For example, copper will eat away aluminum, and bronze will devour zinc.

Important boat fittings are protected from galvanic corrosion with sacrificial zinc blocks, which will be eaten away in preference. They must be replaced regularly.

Corrosion can take place out of the water, too, when different metals touch each other, though a lot more slowly. Stainless steel screws will corrode aluminum spars, for instance, if they're not somehow electrically isolated.

TIP: Bonding all large metal fittings with heavy copper wire is one way to control corrosion. The wire should be grounded at the potential of the surrounding water and firmly fastened to a large zinc.

(See Zinc blocks)

EMERGENCY GEAR

■ Epoxy and duct tape fix almost everything temporarily

Conscientious owners of cruising boats make sure they have tools and materials to cope with all possible emergencies. Some carry specialized gadgets for once-in-a-lifetime accidents, such as the umbrella-like contrivance that you can poke through a hole in the hull from the inside, then open up to cover the hole.

But the trouble with safety gear that's good only for one unlikely purpose is that it gets stowed away in the most inaccessible locker. And if you're anything like me, you'll never remember where it is when panic sets in.

The real emergency equipment boils down to things like duct tape, epoxy putty, thin wire, and nylon ratchet ties. When I accidentally stabbed my inflatable, it was duct tape that kept it afloat. You can always find the duct tape. Duct tape will repair sails, hold splints around a broken tiller, and keep an alligator's mouth closed, should one blunder aboard.

Fast-setting epoxy glue and putty will repair breaks in wood, metal, and fiberglass. It will set under water to repair hull damage. You can even fix engine parts and leaking exhausts with some epoxies. It's magic stuff.

TIP: Don't forget the old trick of using a nylon stocking when an engine belt breaks. It could get you home.

ENGINE POWER

■ **Even with a bigger engine, your boat won't necessarily go faster**

When you're new to sailboats, it takes a while to get used to their slow speed under power. Kindergarten kids can run faster than a sailboat can motor.

Unless you have a planing hull, it's all a matter of maximum hull speed being limited by waterline length. The formula that defines the maximum speed of a wave also applies to displacement hulls, because they dig themselves into a wave at speed, and can't rise out of it. The formula is the square root of waterline length in feet, times 1.34. So a boat with a waterline length of 25 feet has a hull speed of 6.7 knots.

Now it doesn't matter how much more horsepower you add to your engine, you're not going to go much faster than your hull speed. In fact, excessive horsepower would only make the stern squat, maybe enough to flood the cockpit. About 4 horsepower for each ton (2,000 pounds) of boat weight will enable you to reach hull speed in most conditions.

TIP: Although it may seem ludicrous to fit a 30-foot sailboat with a 25-horsepower engine when your car develops 250 horsepower, it actually makes sense. Sailboats are really pretty but they're very slow. Get used to it.

ENGINES, ACCESSIBILITY

■ **You need a miniature contortionist with five-foot arms to service the engine**

It would be hard to imagine a worse place for an engine than the aft bilge of a sailboat. Builders bolt down a bridge-deck and cockpit floor an inch or two above it. Then they seal the whole thing off with bulkheads and companionway steps. So, even if you can remove the steps, you have no access to some of the most important parts of the engine unless you're built like a daddy-longlegs.

Sailboat engines are poorly maintained because you can't get near them. I can't even see the oil dipstick on my engine. It's underneath, around the corner, at the back of the engine in the pitch dark somewhere. I have to grope for it. Getting it back into its little hole is even worse. I'm terrified of dropping it into the bilge under the engine.

I blame yacht designers for this. Few of them give serious thought to engine maintenance. It ought to be possible to use hinged or removable panels to provide access, even if you have to swing the whole galley over your head. Good engine access is vital. It deserves much more attention.

TIP: If you have a quarterberth, see if you can cut an access panel in the engineroom bulkhead.

ENGINES, BLEEDING

■ **Learn to bleed your diesel**

If you spend much time around boats, the chances are that sooner or later you'll have to bleed a diesel. That is, you'll have to purge the fuel system of air.

It might seem strange, but a small bubble of air can prevent a diesel engine from firing. That's because fuel is injected into the cylinder under very high pressure. But air is compressible, so if air is present instead of fuel, the injector will never open and the engine will never start.

To get rid of the air, you have to loosen the fittings at certain connections and physically pump the fuel through until all the air is forced out. It takes time and it can be messy.

Some diesel engines are supposedly self-bleeding. They have electric fuel pumps that will circulate the fuel and send the air out, but even they might require you to crack the injector nuts from time to time.

You'll find detailed instructions in the workshop manual for your engine. Practice, because there may not be time to start learning when your engine quits.

TIP: Be cautious about running the engine when the boat is heeled under sail. The fuel can run to one side of the tank and the engine will suck in air.

ENGINES, CLEAN FUEL

■ **Little bugs can stop big diesel engines**

Diesel engines are known for their rugged reliability but there's one little pest they're very vulnerable to, and that's algae. These tiny organisms from the vegetable kingdom form a sludge in diesel fuel. They quickly clog the filters and prevent fuel from getting to the engine.

But how does algae get into diesel fuel? It grows in fuel tanks. In fact, it *thrives* when conditions are right, which is when fresh water is present in the tank.

And how does fresh water get into a fuel tank? Among other ways, it condenses there. When temperatures cool, the moisture in the air condenses and drains to the bottom of the tank. It doesn't ever evaporate from there because it's covered by a thick layer of fuel. With repeated heating and cooling cycles, a large amount of water can collect in the tank, and algae can flourish.

The answer is to add a biocide to the fuel with every filling of the tank, and to use filters that trap water as well as dirt and other material. It's worthwhile noting that the primary cause of diesel engine problems is contaminated fuel.

TIP: Make a point of inspecting and changing filters frequently. Nothing staves off engine failure better.

ENGINES, FUEL CONSUMPTION

■ It's hard to get the truth about fuel consumption

If you think fuel-mileage figures on new-car stickers are misleading, wait till you to try to find out how many miles you get to the gallon on a boat.

Few boat owners know their fuel consumption to any degree of accuracy because it varies so much with boatspeed, headwinds, contrary currents, and the boat's load. Most owners tend to exaggerate their mileage figures, probably because the truth is so depressing.

Nevertheless, it's important for any serious boater to know at least roughly how far the boat will go on a tankful of fuel, and a couple of simple formulas will help establish that figure.

Firstly, an inboard gasoline engine will use one gallon of fuel per hour for every 10 horsepower expended. So, if a 40-horsepower engine is running at half speed and expending 20 horsepower, it's using about two gallons of fuel every hour.

Diesel fuel has more energy, by volume, than gasoline, so a diesel engine needs about one gallon per hour for every 18 horsepower expended.

Incidentally, most marine engines expend about 75 percent of maximum horsepower at cruising speed.

TIP: Plan to use one-third of your fuel on the outward leg, one-third to get back, and one-third for a safety reserve.

ENGINES, GASOLINE

■ **Gasoline engines still have many advantages over diesel**

You'd be hard pressed to find a new sailboat that comes with an inboard gasoline engine these days. There's a fad for diesel engines. It's based more on unreasonable fear than logic, because modern gasoline engines have many advantages.

The reason most often offered for preferring diesel to gas is that gasoline will explode if it leaks into the bilge. But, ironically, the liquid petroleum gas used in the great majority of boat galleys is just as dangerous, and who complains about that?

You'll find gasoline engines in many thousands of boats because it's a perfectly safe fuel if you take the recommended precautions. Gas engines are unquestionably superior to diesel engines in many ways. A diesel is more expensive, more difficult to fix, and costlier to maintain. It's heavier, noisier, more sluggish, and rougher-running. If you've ever driven a diesel car, you'll understand the difference. Gas engines like the old Atomic 4 were specially designed for boats, but no modern diesel that I know of was.

One advantage of the diesel is that you get more miles per tankful, but bigger tanks or spare cans will fix that.

TIP: Sniff before starting a gasoline engine. The human nose can detect minute quantities of gasoline in air.

ENGINES, LIFE EXPECTANCY

■ **You can expect 5,000 hours of good service from a diesel engine**

Diesel engines were designed for long periods of hard work. Most boat diesels started off as tractor engines or powerplants for generators and other heavy equipment. They're not particularly suited to short periods of use at low power, such as they often get on auxiliary sailboats. Nevertheless, their robust construction and precise engineering give them long lives.

Ashore, a diesel engine in a big truck may run for 1,000,000 miles before needing a major overhaul. In a fishing boat that stays at sea for long periods, you can expect 8,000 trouble-free hours. In an auxiliary yacht, that figure comes down to an average of about 5,000 hours with good maintenance. As the average private sailboat is under power for about 200 hours a year, that's 25 years worth of use.

An equivalent gasoline engine, by contrast, will probably run for only 1,500 hours before needing an overhaul. It will likely get about 1,000 hours of perfect operation and then start experiencing minor trouble for the next 500 hours. But the costs tend to even out because the gas engine is cheaper to buy and repair.

TIP: Try to run your diesel at near full throttle under full load for 10 or 15 minutes every time you use it.

ENGINES, OPERATING

■ **We rarely give engines the things they need most**

On most sailboats, the auxiliary engine is crowded into a tiny space that makes access difficult. So we rarely give our engines the things they desire most. But no matter what trouble you have to go to, there are certain essential maintenance checks that you *must* make.

Oil: check the level every day, and don't overfill. Check the color, too. On a diesel, it should be jet black after a few hours' use. On a gas engine it will stay cleaner longer. Once a month or so, check the level of the gearbox oil, too.

Air: engines like lots of clean cool air. They rarely get it. Make sure those air-supply hoses haven't been flattened by someone lying on them.

Water: check the coolant level every day. Be sure it has enough anti-freeze. Check that the raw-water impeller has all its blades and is still flexible. Every time you start the engine, check for water coming out of the exhaust.

Filters: inspect your fuel filters and water separator for signs of algae or excess water.

Also keep an eye on the electrolyte level in your batteries if they're the lead-acid type.

TIP: A *rising* oil level can mean water is getting into it. Big trouble.

ENGINES, RUNAWAY

■ **Nothing is more frightening than a runaway diesel**

You're about as likely to meet a runaway diesel as you are to have a beer with the Pope. But the fact that some engine manufacturers provide special equipment for shutting down a runaway diesel indicates that the problem really does exist.

Luckily, it's very rare because a runaway diesel is a bomb about to explode. It's racing ever faster and none of your usual controls will stop it. It's not running on diesel fuel, but on oil getting past a seal or coming from an overfilled oil pan. It's roaring and vibrating and getting ready to blow a piston through the cylinder head with the force of a landmine.

You can stop it with a carbon dioxide fire extinguisher aimed at the air intake. Failing that, you must block the air intake physically. How you do that depends on the construction of your engine. A piece of plywood or plastic might work. Some people advocate that you push a soft ball against the air inlet, but that's not good for every engine. On some engines, there's a sliding gate to cut off the air supply.

TIP: Find out where your air intake is and figure out the best way to cut off the air.

ENGINES, SURVEYING

■ What a good mechanic can tell you about a used engine

It has always seemed strange to me that marine surveyors don't survey some of the most important parts of a boat. Hardly any will investigate the condition of the auxiliary engine.

The engine represents a large portion of the value of a sailboat. A new one professionally installed costs as much as a small car. If you're buying a used boat, therefore, it will pay you to get a good mechanic to survey the engine.

A well-equipped mechanic can use a heat sensor to check for blocked water passages, a bad thermostat, and other cooling problems. A compression test will uncover bad rings or worn cylinders. Smoke, steam, and water coming from the exhaust all tell their own stories to the expert and an electrical test will determine the state of the batteries and the amount of charge from the alternator.

A good mechanic will check the fuel filters for signs of water and

algae in the fuel tank. Engine alignment, the condition of hoses, the color of the engine oil, the amount of corrosion, the condition of the engine mounts—all these things should be checked. It's money well spent.

TIP: Not every mechanic has the equipment needed for a thorough survey. Make sure yours has.

ENGINES, TOOLS

■ Be prepared to work on your engine

Even if you know nothing about engines, be prepared to carry out routine maintenance on your auxiliary. Professional mechanics are expensive because they inevitably have to work in dark, awkward spaces with hardly enough room to swing a wrench. Often they must *invent* ways of getting a job done, and they rarely enjoy the conditions available to their colleagues in nice workshops on shore.

So you should be able to do all the maintenance without help: oil changes, filter changes, zinc changes, bleeding fuel lines, battery maintenance, changing the raw-water impeller, and so on. Faithful maintenance will keep most engines running almost indefinitely. You shouldn't have to resort to calling in a mechanic until there are signs that serious engine surgery is needed.

You'll need a set of tools and the correct filters, gaskets, and spare parts. It's a modest outlay that will save you a lot of money in the long run. Better still, being able to tackle these jobs will make you feel much more in control, much more confident to analyze problems and solve emergencies.

None of the maintenance work requires much technical knowledge. So screw up your courage and start.

TIP: Buy the owner's manual *and* the workshop manual. They're worth their weight in gold.

ENGINES, UNNECESSARY

■ **You can sail around the world without an engine**

Weekend sailors and coastal sailors need auxiliary engines. If you're tied to schedules on shore, you have to get back on time when the wind drops.

But if you're planning to cross an ocean or sail around the world, you don't need an engine at all, just a lot of patience and maybe a dash of luck when anchoring or docking.

Many small boats have sailed across oceans and around the world without engines. Even today, Lin and Larry Pardey still do it in their 29-foot cutter *Taleisin*, and they're not alone.

There are many advantages. One of the greatest is the amount of room you gain down below. Engines take up a lot of space. It's not just the engine itself, but the associated tanks, hoses, wires, filters exhaust pipe, instrument panel, batteries, cockpit controls, and propeller shaft.

No engine also means less expense, less weight, no waiting for spare parts, two fewer holes through the hull, no oily bilges, faster sailing without prop drag, and no ulcers from constant fretting over whether the engine will start or not when you really *need* the damn thing.

TIP: They won't let you sail through the Panama Canal, but you can borrow or hire an outboard motor to make the transit.

ENGINES, UNRELIABLE

■ **Engines don't always run when you want them to**

Marine engines seem to get more reliable all the time but they still have their off-days. Too many of them are victims of poor mainte-nance and difficult working conditions, but even on the best-regulated boats, batteries go flat, filters become blocked, and fuel goes bad.

So never trust your engine. It could quit at any time.

Always have your sails ready for instant hoisting when you leave your mooring or marina slip. Practice maneuvers such as anchoring and docking under sail, just in case.

Remember, too, that a dinghy with an outboard makes a nice little tug to guide you through tight fairways. If you really get serious and learn the ancient Chinese art of sculling over the stern with an oar you will, of course, ensure that your engine never ever fails.

But if it does, and you're hesitant to enter a marina under sail, call "any boat in so-and-so marina" on VHF Channel 16 and ask if anyone has an outboard dinghy that could tow you in the last hundred yards. Or, be a moocher and beg a tow from a passing boat.

TIP: If you sail into the close quarters of a marina, keep two anchors ready for instant casting, one astern and one at the bow.

FEAR

■ Anxiety is a frequent and natural part of boating

Part of the attraction of sailing is that it frightens the pants off you now and then. Those of us who spend most of our lives cosseted in the comforts of civilization seem to crave the occasional brush with a manageable slice of terror, the better by contrast to appreciate those comforts. So we go sailing, we get a little scared, and everyone's happy.

The trouble is the anticipation, the waiting for the terror to come. We call that anxiety. It affects most sailors some of the time, and while psychologists say it's natural, and nothing to worry about, beginners often wonder if sailing requires audacity and heroism they don't possess.

Not so. Anxiety is Nature's way of keeping you safe. It sharpens your senses and whets your survival instincts, so that you are prepared when danger arrives in the form of a line squall or a fog bank filled with ocean-going freighters.

Were it not for anxiety, beginners might blunder unknowingly into danger and find themselves frozen with fear. A good dose of apprehension forces them to take the precautions an experienced sailor takes without giving it a thought.

TIP: Apprehension before a voyage often disappears the moment you get under way, and always diminishes with experience.

(See Hallucinations; Voices from the sea)

FOG

■ You won't believe how bad fog is until you get caught in it

Fog is awful. Panic is never far off when fog wraps its clammy blanket around you and blinds you.

With fog comes a tense edginess. Your ears take over from your eyes. Your sense of hearing unwillingly assumes the vital task of keeping the ship and crew safe, a responsibility it can't handle.

Things move stealthily in that misty cloud. But no matter how hard you stare, your eyes won't reveal what perils it's hiding. That "whoosh-whoosh-whoosh" noise sounds like a huge propeller on a really big ship. But you can't tell which way it's heading. You can't tell anything. Your normal senses have no validity.

You blow your horn, a ritual gesture to ward off danger, and then you hear a heart-stopping response from nearby. Omigod, what is it? What does one long, two short mean? Are you passing between a tug and her tow? Are you about to get tangled in a fishing boat's gill net? Should you stop? Should you reverse course at full speed? The mind reels. Fog is awful.

TIP: Lacking a radar set, your best protection in fog is a GPS receiver to know your position, a VHF radio to broadcast it, and a radar reflector hoisted as high in the rigging as possible.

(See Avoiding collisions; Radar; Radar reflectors)

FORECASTING WEATHER

■ **A barometer is about as good as a weatherfax**

Weather forecasting is an inexact science. Forecasters don't often admit it, but few forecasts are accurate for more than three days ahead. And no wonder.

Weather is just great spheres of air, huge warm and cold bubbles hundreds or thousands of miles across, jostling fiercely against each other, moving up and down. Who knows where they might go next? If you find yourself at the meeting point of two bubbles (what the experts call a front) you can expect some very interesting weather as they try to beat each other up.

Your barometer measures the atmospheric pressure inside these bubbles. High pressure means a good bubble and nice weather. Low pressure signifies a bad bubble and rotten weather.

So if your barometer is steady, you can expect tomorrow's weather to be much more like today's than anything else. If it's falling, you can expect bad weather. The faster the fall, the sooner it will arrive. If the glass is rising, a good bubble has arrived and fine weather will follow.

You'll find your barometer just as reliable as a weatherfax once you've learnt to interpret it, and a lot cheaper.

TIP: It's the *speed* of the barometer's rise or fall that determines how quickly and how drastically the weather will change.

FREAK WAVES

■ **Killer waves are more common than we thought**

The European Space Agency has confirmed that freak waves exist "in higher numbers than anyone expected." Wolfgang Rosenthal, senior scientist with the GKSS Research Center in Geesthacht, Germany, says two of the agency's Earth-scanning satellites used radar to monitor the oceans for three weeks. They identified more than 10 individual giant waves around the globe that were more than 25 meters (81.25 feet) high.

Laurence Draper, of the British National Institute of Oceanography, has long insisted it's no old wives' tale that every fifth, or seventh, or ninth wave is larger than the others. Sea systems are composed of many different wave trains, he says, each with its own speed and height.

So, at random intervals, waves can ride on each other's backs to form an exceptionally high wave—and it doesn't have to be blowing hard. Draper estimates that one wave in 23 is twice the average height; one in 1,175 is three times higher; and one in 300,000 is more than four times higher.

But it's the height of the breaking crest that's the greatest threat to small sailboats. Luckily, the size of the crest does not necessarily relate to the size of the wave in deep open water.

TIP: Beware of strong ocean currents, where contrary winds create the biggest and steepest waves.

(See Capsize; Wave heights)

FRESHWATER SUPPLIES

■ There's never enough fresh water on a boat

Boats never carry enough fresh water for the likes of their crews. Water is simply too heavy and bulky to waste on daily showers and washing clothes. Only really big vessels have sufficient tankage for those purposes, so we lesser mortals have to struggle along with a lick here and a spit there.

There are machines that make fresh water from the sea, which would seem to be the answer, but they're beyond the resources of most of us, simply too expensive to buy and maintain.

Many long-distance cruisers manage to catch enough rain to keep their tanks topped up. Some collect rainwater in a bucket where it runs in a stream off the mainsail at the gooseneck. Others plug the cockpit drains and siphon the water into the tanks below. If you have an upright dinghy on deck it could also be an extra catchment area.

You should let the first few minutes of a rainstorm wash away the dirt from sails and decks before you start collecting, of course, if you need drinking water. Otherwise, you can use slightly tainted water for showers or washing clothes.

TIP: You can often scoop fresh water off the surface of the sea after heavy rain in calm conditions. It floats on top of the denser salt water.

(See Drinking seawater; Freshwater supplies; Water)

G

GPS

■ It's an electronic miracle, but it isn't always accurate

Don't be misled by the fact that the Global Positioning System (GPS) can fix your boat's position to within 30 feet or less anywhere in the world. That won't help you if the coordinates of latitude and longitude used by the GPS aren't the same as the ones used by your chartmaker.

And in many cases, they aren't. When you plot your GPS coordinates on a chart, they can be a mile or more in error. That's because different surveys over the centuries used different base references. Because the Earth isn't a perfect sphere, no one grid of latitude and longitude will touch the face of the globe everywhere.

Most GPS receivers made for boats allow you to change the survey base to the one mentioned on your chart, in which case the GPS will show your correct position relative to that chart.

GPS is the biggest advance in nautical navigation since the discovery of the magnetic compass. It has proved extremely reliable, despite the fact that the U.S. Department of Defense, which operates it, has deliberately degraded its accuracy for private users in the past.

TIP: Use GPS to make a landfall. Then, as soon as you can, fix your position by bearings from the shore.

(See Navigation aids)

GROUNDING

▪ **Sooner or later, you'll run aground**

Most experienced sailors have been aground at one time or another. The chances are that you will go aground, too.

The severity of damage depends on many factors, including the state of the sea. A full-keel yacht usually suffers less structural damage from the initial impact than does a fin-keeled boat. The sloping full keel rides up and absorbs the shock gradually. Obviously, running onto sand is better than running onto rock, and smooth rock is better than jagged rock.

When you're stopped suddenly by rock, first check for crew injuries. Then look in the bilges. If water is pouring in faster than your pumps can handle it, you have this choice: 1. If you're not stuck on the rock, try to run your boat ashore before she sinks; 2. Put out a Mayday call and prepare to abandon ship.

On sand, pebbles or mud, try to spin around and face deep water. Send out an anchor and winch her off, or arrange a tow when the tide rises.

TIP: Reduce her draft by pumping out your fresh water and putting heavy objects into the dinghy. A second anchor attached to the masthead by the main halyard will reduce draft by heeling her over.

H

HALLUCINATIONS

■ **Sailors hallucinate at sea and hear voices**

One of the problems sailors experience on long trips is lack of sleep. For singlehanders it's a chronic problem of course, but even on well-manned boats some crewmembers have difficulty adjusting to watch systems that require them to sleep during the day and work at night. Industrial psychologists ashore say that some factory workers take a week to adjust to new schedules—and some never really do adjust. The same applies to yacht crews on ocean voyages.

Lack of sleep robs you of the deep dreams that are an important part of mental health. But your brain has a mechanism that takes over when mental fatigue threatens to overwhelm safety. Your mind invents "waking dreams" in the form of hallucinations or illusions.

There are well-documented cases of sailors believing they have entered port and dropped anchor after a long, exhausting bout with a gale at sea. But when they wake up after collapsing for 12 hours on the cabin floor, they invariably find themselves still at sea with no land in sight—yet the sails are stowed and the anchor is hanging over the bow without touching bottom.

TIP: Some people also hear voices, but doctors say all these sleep-deprived hallucinations are harmless in the long run.

(See Fear; Voices from the sea)

HEADROOM

■ **Standing room down below comes at a price**

It's generally accepted that full standing headroom in a boat is 6 feet 1 inch, but few sailboats under 27 feet in length can provide it without resorting to a tall and ugly cabin trunk.

There are several troubling aspects to a high deckhouse besides the aesthetic shock. It creates wind resistance, for a start, which is particularly disadvantageous when you're sailing against the wind. It's also more prone to damage by large waves.

Furthermore, it's dangerous to work at the base of the mast when handling the mainsail because you're poised comparatively high over the water for the width of the boat. If she's sharply heeled you could fall overboard without touching the lifelines.

Heavy-displacement boats can get away with lower, sleeker cabin trunks because their cabin soles extend farther below the waterline, but there is no alternative on a light-displacement hull (if full headroom is required) than to build upward.

But you really only need standing headroom when you're not sailing. Under way, you spend your time mostly sitting down or lying down. And you can always go on deck. Plenty of headroom up there.

TIP: Good sitting headroom is 4 feet 9 inches. Anything between that and full standing headroom is truly a pain in the neck.

HIDDEN MYSTERIES

■ **Boats are full of hidden mysteries**

Your newly acquired boat may look perfectly normal on the outside. But as soon as you start lifting hatches, opening lockers, pulling drawers, and peering into the engine compartment, an enigmatic new world will emerge.

It can take you months to discover how all the systems work, where all the seacocks are, and why the masthead light only comes on if you plug in the cabin fan as well.

Boat owners are a meddlesome lot. They can't resist adding or altering things in their constant quest for perfection.

The engine compartment glows eerily with pale LEDs the previous owner failed to explain. They dimly outline a puzzling forest of pipes, wires, and levers. Under a companionway step, a lump of something grows a white fur coat with startling orange spots. Deep in the bilge a loose copper wire terminates in a halo of virulent green fuzz.

A bikini top lies insolently at the foot of the quarterberth and a sticky drawer delivers a crumpled receipt for repairs to bottom blisters you weren't told about. Gradually, one-by-one, you will solve the mysteries. You just need patience.

TIP: Make notes while you sit down with the previous owner and go through everything from stem to stern.

HOBBYHORSING

■ **This bad habit can destroy performance**

When a sailboat going to windward comes to a standstill, pitching and scending in the same place, she's said to be hobbyhorsing. This lack of progress is greatly exacerbated by a phenomenon called inertia. It's the tendency of a moving body to want to continue moving in the same direction at the same speed, and also the tendency of a body at rest to resist being moved.

Heavy weights at a distance from a boat's center of buoyancy contribute a lot to inertia, particularly if they're in the bows or stern. So if you move those weights in toward the fore-and-aft center of the boat she will tend to ride buoyantly over the waves instead of plunging too deeply into them.

There's always the chance, of course, of taking things too far. If the ride becomes too violent, you may stress the rig unfairly, not to mention the crew. So you have to experiment. Like everything else on a boat, this cure is a compromise. Move some weights back toward the extremities until you find a reasonable middle course between hobbyhorsing and slamming.

TIP: A heavy mast is full of inertia. Do all you can to lighten it, especially up high where the leverage is greatest.

(See Inertia)

HOLDING VALUE

■ Some boats don't hold their resale value

The market value of some boats drops quicker than others. This often comes as an unwelcome surprise when it's time to sell your boat.

Here are some of the things about sailboats that give them good resale value:

Fiberglass hulls; first-class workmanship from reputable manufacturers; white hulls; conservative rigs; good sails; expensive fittings; clean diesel engines with low hours; sweet-smelling cabins and lockers; dry clean bilges; good ventilation; pretty sheerlines; low coachhouses; and bronze seacocks.

Here are some of the things that lower a boat's resale value:

Hulls of steel, concrete, or wood (with the exception of modern wood/epoxy construction); one-off racing hulls; blistered gel coat; flimsy construction; a reputation for weather helm; hull colors other than white; experimental rigs; blown-out sails; cheap fittings; neglected gasoline engines; musty smells down below; worn upholstery; dirty, wet, oily bilges; lack of ventilation; unknown designers; ugly deckhouses; in-mast or in-boom reefing; centerboards; unusually skinny or beamy hulls; gate valves instead of seacocks; rust anywhere; and smelly heads.

The resale value of the average 10-year-old steel boat declines by about 50 percent, and ferro-concrete hulls slightly more.

TIP: When you want to sell, move all your personal gear off and scrub everything spotlessly clean.

HYPOTHERMIA

■ The water doesn't have to be very cold to kill you

Don't get the idea that only excessively cold water will kill you if you fall overboard. You can actually get hypothermia, in which the body's core temperature is lowered to fatal levels, in tropical waters if you stay in long enough.

In fact, in areas where the summertime water temperature is about 65°F, as it is over much of the United States, you could lapse into frigid unconsciousness in about two hours. Be aware of the signs: violent shivering, blue lips, and slurred speech.

Some people succumb quicker than others, of course, depending, among other things, upon whether they're skinny or have a protective layer of fat.

It's tempting to keep moving vigorously in the water to keep warm, but unfortunately that's the quickest way to lose body heat. Experts always advise you to huddle in a heat-preserving position and keep your head and extremities covered if possible. If there is flotsam around, do your best to get your body out of the water, even partially.

TIP: Don't give hypothermia victims alcohol or stimulants such as coffee or tea and don't massage arms or legs. Provide only gentle heating. Warm them gradually by sharing a sleeping bag with them and blowing your warm breath into victims' mouths as they breathe.

I-K

ICE ON BOARD

■ Making ice calls for a lot of power

The tinkle of ice in a tall glass is an entrancing sound. It's especially delightful when you're safely at anchor in a pretty cove after a hard day's sail. But it takes a surprising amount of power to make ice on a small boat.

Weekend sailors mostly make do with ice-boxes, but long-distance cruisers often opt for on-board refrigeration.

The two most common methods are engine-driven compressors feeding supercooled fluid to metal holding plates in an ice-box, and modified household fridges running on 12-volt motors. Holding-plate systems are expensive to start with, and require you to run the ship's engine for about two hours every day. Fridge systems cost about one-third less, but the electrical draw is heavy and constant.

Your 12-volt batteries will need to provide about 4 amp-hours of power for every hour of refrigerating—almost 100 amp-hours a day—in hot climates. That's a lot for the average cruiser to replenish, even if the auxiliary engine is running an extra-large alternator. And then there's the noise of the fridge motor cycling on and off all day and night.

One way or another, you pay dearly for ice.

TIP: Learn to maintain your system. There are no repair shops at sea.

INERTIA

■ **It's bad for you, good for a sailboat**

Inertia comes in very useful on small sailboats. It helps prevent capsize.

The physical property known as inertia prevents *sudden* reaction to a force acting on a boat. Thus, if a large breaking wave hits a hull broadside-on, that boat will not immediately be thrown over onto her beam ends.

Boats with inertia include those with heavy displacement and deep, full keels. According to the distinguished research scientist and naval architect Tony Marchaj, beamy, light displacement, fin-keeled boats of the same length are five times more likely to be capsized by wave impact.

But inertia has its downside, too. The heavy mast that prevents jerky movement in choppy seas will also tend to extend the arc of rolling downwind. That's because inertia also resists slowing and change of direction in a body that's already moving.

The disposition of weights on a small boat can modify this effect of inertia. Moving them away from the ends of the boat toward the center, for example, will decrease hobbyhorsing.

TIP: The longer, deeper, heavier, and narrower a boat, length for length, the more inertia she possesses, and therefore more resistance to wave-impact capsize. This resistance increases greatly with length, so a good big boat is more seaworthy than a good little boat.

(See Hobbyhorsing; Seakindliness)

KEEL DESIGN

■ Fin-keelers sail around the world, too

You'll often hear that the only suitable deep-sea cruiser is one with a traditional full keel. That's the type found on heavy-displacement Colin Archers and Bristol Channel cutters. But that totally overlooks the fact that fin-keeled boats cross oceans all the time. It also overlooks the fact that the only boat in her class to finish the 1979 Fastnet Race in England was a fin-keeler, a 32-foot Contessa named ASSENT. Five boats sank in that race, and 19 were abandoned.

Contessas have circumnavigated, and rounded Cape Horn the "wrong" way. And they're not the only fin-keelers out on the open ocean, of course. Even a 27-foot Catalina called JUGGERNAUT was sailed around the world singlehanded by Patrick Childress of Rhode Island.

In general, I'd say that a full-keeled boat will look after herself better in heavy weather when the fatigued crew needs to go below. A fin-keeler demands more attention, and often should be sailed rather than hove-to or lain ahull, so that the dynamic forces trying to overturn her can be better dissipated by a keel of relatively small area being moved through more water.

TIP: The skill and experience of the crew contribute more to survival than the difference between a full keel and a fin keel.

(See Seaworthiness)

KNOTS

■ Tying a knot reduces the strength of a line

It's important to realize that sharp kinks in a rope detract from its strength. Even worse, if you stress a three-strand rope with a sharp kink to its full working load or more, that rope will have lost about 30 percent of its strength for ever.

Every time you tie a knot in a line, you obviously introduce tight kinks that distort the fibers, but some knots have tighter kinks than others. So different knots reduce the strength of rope by different amounts.

Of the most commonly used knots, the anchor bend causes the least destruction to the line's fibers. It reduces the line's strength by only 24 percent. One of the worst knots to use is the reef knot, which robs a rope of a whopping 55 percent of its strength.

In between those two we find the following strength losses for various knots: timber hitch, 30 to 35 percent; round turn and two half-hitches, 30 to 35 percent; bowline, 40 percent; clove hitch, 40 percent; sheet bend, 45 percent.

Modern line is very strong but it's important to know its limits when it's knotted.

TIP: Good eye splices and short splices hardly detract from a line's strength at all, so use them wherever you can.

L

LEAKS

■ Every boat leaks, even fiberglass ones

You'd think it almost impossible for a fiberglass boat to leak. After all it's built like an eggshell. Where would water get in?

Just about everywhere, actually. The trouble is that fiberglass hulls have holes in them. In most cases, the number of holes is comparatively small—dozens or scores—but in others it can be in the hundreds.

Most boats have large fittings that let fluids pass right through the hull, in and out. The engine cooling water comes in that way, for example, as does flushing water for the head. The galley sink drains that way. The through-hull fittings are bedded in compounds to prevent leaks, but as boats age the compound shifts, oozes out, or becomes more brittle, allowing water to enter. Old seacocks often leak, too.

All boats have holes through the deck and cabintop for various fittings and some have hundreds of holes for screws holding down strips of teak decking. In theory, all these holes are sealed. In practice, many will leak when it rains or when spray hits the deck.

TIP: Tracing the source of a leak is notoriously difficult. The best way is to seal the boat and pump in air at low pressure. Brush soapy water over the superstructure and watch for bubbles.

LEARNING THE ROPES

■ **You don't have to learn the names of all the ropes immediately**

Some boat owners like to show off their knowledge by using technical terms that beginners can't understand. They give the impression that you can't sail, or even crew efficiently, if you're not familiar with nautical jargon.

That's not true, of course. You only have to see the kindergartners sailing the Optimists to know that. In fact, the more a skipper insists on pompous correctitude, the less likely he or she is to be a capable and experienced mariner.

Sailor's lingo was important in the heyday of sail, when sailing ships had hundreds of lines and sailors had to know each one by name. But those times are past. If you're a beginner, you can pick up the right terms at your own pace now.

Skippers whose self-importance exceeds their knowledge often insist that when rope is taken aboard a vessel, it becomes line. Not so. There are several kinds of ropes, including bolt ropes and foot ropes. And guess what sailors said of a hand who showed professional competence? They said he knew the ropes. And nobody ever boasted that he knew the lines.

TIP: If you're a skipper, always repeat the correct phrase after giving a simplified one, so that novices learn the sailor's lingo quickly and naturally.

LEARNING TO SAIL

■ Almost anybody can learn to sail in an hour

Put a kid in a small sailing dinghy and see what happens. Within minutes, he or she has figured out how to work the three main controls—tiller, mainsheet, and daggerboard.

Even an adult can learn to sail in an hour or less. To tell the truth, basic survival sailing comes almost instinctively to most people. There are exceptions, of course, people who can't get the hang of where the wind is coming from, or who panic when the boat starts to heel. But on the whole, sailing is a pretty simple pastime.

On a typical professionally taught sailing course over a weekend, you'll learn the rules of the road, elementary navigation, crew overboard drills, coast-guard safety requirements, light and sound signals, anchoring and docking procedures, and a whole lot of other stuff apart from the simple skills of sailing.

What we call *sailing* actually involves many disciplines, from weather forecasting to domestic science, but the nub of it all, the actual business of making a small boat travel though water in the right direction, is not complicated. If you can drive a car, you can certainly sail a boat.

TIP: It's best to learn the basics in a boat of 25 feet or less. Then you'll be ready to sail anything.

(See Sailing skill)

LEEWAY

■ **Like the poor, leeway is always with us**

Leeway is the slight sideways movement of a sailboat through the water. It's present on all courses except dead downwind.

It's fascinating to think that without leeway a boat could make no progress to windward. The slight angle that the keel makes to the straight line of forward progress results in a hydrodynamic "lift." That counteracts the sideways push of the sails.

In this respect, a sailboat's keel is the nautical equivalent of an airplane wing and, like the wing, it needs to present a slight angle to the medium it travels through.

Unlike an airplane's wing, however, a sailboat's keel cannot be permanently angled to the flow of fluid. The keel has to provide "lift" on both tacks. It is therefore placed in a straight line fore and aft, and the necessary angle is made by turning the whole boat and keel as a unit. In other words, the boat and keel drag slightly sideways through the water. Without the keel, the boat would blow off to leeward much more severely and progress to windward would be very poor.

TIP: In a light breeze, the average close-hauled sailboat will make 4 or 5 degrees of leeway; in a 20-knot breeze, as much as 8 degrees.

LIES

■ **People always lie about how fast their boats are**

Always take sailors' estimates of their boats' speed with a dose of salt. They lie. Mostly not deliberately, although you probably know a couple who do. The trouble is that boat speed is very difficult to measure exactly.

Knotmeters are only as good as their calibration—often pure guesswork. GPS is notoriously unreliable for speeds and doesn't account for current.

For accuracy, time your progress over a known distance. For example, to determine your maximum speed under power, find a measured nautical mile. Many are marked on large-scale charts, but you can also use landmarks to measure your own.

- On a calm day, time the boat in seconds between the marks.
- Divide the number of seconds into 3,600. The answer is your speed in knots.
- Reverse your course and time the run between the marks. Find the speed again.
- Average the two speeds. (Not the two times.) The result is your true speed through the water.
- Steam at top speed as before, and calibrate your knotmeter.
- Repeat the speed trial in both directions to check the accuracy of your knotmeter and the distance log.

TIP: The measured course must be in water of about 30 feet or deeper. Shallow water causes a drag and slows your boat.

(See Speed)

LIFE RAFTS

■ Ask yourself if a life raft will do you any good

Before you rush out and hand over thousands of dollars for a life raft, ask yourself a simple question: What are the chances of a tiny, fragile life raft surviving a storm that sank a much bigger and more seaworthy boat?

Not all that good, apparently. In a famous storm during a Fastnet Race off England in 1979, seven sailors lost their lives because of what an official board of enquiry described as "failure of the life rafts." The board noted further: "life rafts clearly failed to provide the safe refuge which many crews expected."

In the Queen's Birthday Storm off New Zealand in 1994, the *only* three sailors who took to a life raft were lost and never seen again.

Even if a raft survives the ordeal of launching in a storm, its occupants then have to sit and wait to be rescued, which is catastrophic for morale. Psychologists say people are far more likely to survive if they can make progress toward land.

If your boat is big enough to carry one, an unsinkable fiberglass or wooden dinghy is preferable. If not, a partially inflated inflatable dinghy on the cabintop will suffice. Most boats have room for that.

TIP: The overwhelming advice is to stay with your boat until it actually sinks under you.

LIFELINES

■ Never trust your lifelines

Lifelines covered in white plastic look pretty shippy on a sailboat, but don't let them fool you. Few have sufficient strength to prevent a heavy crewmember crashing through and falling overboard.

The trouble is that lifelines are strung from thin vertical poles, called stanchions, that don't have much stability. Stanchions have small bases where they're attached to the deck, and the leverage applied by a falling body is tremendous.

In some cases, lifelines are too low to be effective, and serve only to catch you behind the knee and flip you overboard. If you fall from a high cabintop while the boat's heeled, you could miss the lifelines altogether.

Offshore racing authorities usually require two rows of lifelines each side with a maximum height of at least 24 inches. But 30 inches, which catches most people high on the thigh, is better if the stanchions are well anchored. They must be through-bolted, never screwed, and fitted with large and heavy backing plates underneath to spread the stress load.

Lifelines should be regarded purely as back-up protection. Primary protection comes from strong harnesses attached to substantial fittings, or jackstays, by tethers short enough to keep you on board.

TIP: White plastic coating can hide corrosion, so bare 1 x 19 stainless-steel wire is actually safer.

LIGHTNING

■ Lots of boats get hit by lightning

If you have an auxiliary sailboat, your chances of getting struck by lightning are 6 in 1,000. That figure comes from the insurance claims section of BoatU.S.

It's an actuarial estimate, of course, so in practical terms you're probably much more likely to be struck by lightning in sub-tropical areas such as Florida and the Gulf Coast where thunderstorms are more frequent.

Not many deaths are reported from lightning strikes on boats, but it does happen from time to time. More frequently, the boat's electronics are destroyed and in some cases holes can be blown right through the hull.

Experts recommend you join a metal mast as directly as possible to an underwater metal "ground" at least one square foot in area with thick copper wire—at least #4 AWG. This, they say, provides a cone of protection that attracts and harmlessly grounds static strikes.

Experienced voyagers often run a length of chain over the stern from the backstay during an electrical storm as a backup. They also unplug SSB, VHF, GPS, and loran antennas.

TIP: Avoid contact with all metal on your boat during a thunderstorm. Don't touch the mast, stays, shrouds, pulpit, pushpit, or bare lifelines. If you have a metal steering wheel, wear gloves.

LOG BOOKS

■ You don't need a fancy log book

The object of a log book is to provide a record of a vessel's voyages. It establishes where she was at any time and how she was managed.

Private vessels don't need to keep logs, but ocean voyagers normally make a note of bearings taken to establish fixes, noon positions, wind and sea conditions, and the boat's reaction to them. It's also useful to note daily the remaining reserves of fuel, water and stores.

Despite its simplicity and informality, the log book is a legal document that should be able to withstand scrutiny in a court of law. It should be filled in at the end of each watch. Every page should be signed by the vessel's captain.

But you don't need an expensive, hidebound, gilt-edged log book. A hard-cover, spiral-bound school notebook will do just

fine. Use two pages for each day. Rule your own columns for the time, course steered, the distance-log reading, wind and weather conditions, the barometer reading, and a large column on the right-hand page for any remarks concerning landmarks, sea state, radio transmissions, and so on. Make space at the bottom for your noon position, day's run, and fuel and water reserves.

TIP: If you make a mistake, don't erase. Draw a line through it, correct it, and initial it.

LUCK

■ **You can earn your luck as you go**

Dr. Earle Reynolds, an atomic scientist and small-boat voyager, once listed the four main essentials for successful yacht voyages as:

- A well-found ship
- A good crew
- Adequate preparation and maintenance, and
- Seamanship, or know-how.

But, although he didn't mention it for fear of losing it, he knew there was also a fifth essential. It's one that most of us instinctively recognize as belonging to the list: luck.

There's no doubt that some skippers and some ships seem to be lucky, while others are patently unlucky. Why should this be?

Well, I believe that luck can be earned. Every time you take a seamanlike precaution you build up a reserve of luck. When you take the trouble to buy the right charts, or check that the anchor is properly set, you're earning luck. Your store increases when you do those dirty or awkward chores such as changing the engine oil and filters on time, or servicing and greasing the seacocks.

When you're in trouble, your store of luck will see you through. Boats that don't have a reserve of luck might not fare as well.

TIP: You can use up your store of luck very quickly. Start replenishing your supply as soon as possible because the sea doesn't grant credit.

(See Renaming a Boat; Unlucky names)

M

MAINTENANCE

■ **Sail, and the world sails with you; sand, and you sand alone**

When you're new to sailing, it's not particularly obvious that boats need a lot of maintenance. It usually comes as a shock after you've bought a boat.

If you're rich, you simply hand the boat over to a yard that charges $60 an hour or more for labor. Otherwise, you do it yourself. Every year or two, you have to coat the bottom with antifouling paint. Sounds easy, but before you can paint you have to sand down the old paint, or even strip it all off if many coats have collected over the years.

Be prepared to undertake it on your own. Very few of those Sunday afternoon sailors who are delighted to crew for you are keen to roll up their sleeves, don their dust masks, and sand the copper paint off the hull.

Then there's the varnish, a never-ending task, and servicing the head, a job that never filled anyone with joy. And so many other tedious, messy, uncomfortable, and even dangerous jobs, including greasing the seacocks, changing the engine oil, adjusting the stuffing box, swabbing out the bilge, renewing the spreader boots, and changing the bulb in the masthead light.

Learn to do them all. They're yours.

TIP: You can reduce boatyard charges by doing all the tedious preparation work yourself.

MAINTENANCE, TEAK

■ **You don't *have* to varnish teak**

Teak is a wood greatly favored by boatbuilders for several very good reasons. It's soft, easily worked, and free of knot-holes. It's naturally oily, which makes it almost rot-proof. It weathers to an attractive light gray when it's left untreated, but it turns a spectacular honey-brown when oiled or varnished.

And there's the problem. It looks so good, so shiny and mellow, so smart and yachty, that boat owners find it very difficult to resist varnishing or oiling the outside trim—the cockpit coamings, the gunwale, the handrails, the Dorade boxes, and so on. The result is gorgeous, but the maintenance is constant.

But you don't have to be varnishing when you could be out sailing. You can let your outside teak go gray without harming it. You could clean it once or twice a year with a teak restorer if you want, but it's not usually necessary. In fact, excessive scrubbing harms it by wearing away the softer parts and leaving hard ridges exposed. That can only be cured by sanding it smooth again, and you don't want to do that too often because it removes so much material.

TIP: Varnish your teak only once—just before you put your boat up for sale. Buyers are hopelessly attracted by the beautiful honey glitter.

(See Teak and varnish)

MESSING ABOUT

■ Nothing is half so much worth doing

It took a water rat, in conversation with a mole, to reveal one of the great human truths, which is that "there is *nothing*—absolutely nothing—half so much worth doing as simply messing about in boats."

The famous quote comes, of course, from Kenneth Grahame's dearly loved classic, *The Wind in the Willows*. When Mole shyly revealed that he had never been in a boat before in all his life, Rat, who had offered to scull him across the river, was open-mouthed with astonishment. He was moved to ask: "What have you been doing, then?"

Mole didn't answer. He was experiencing the bliss, the quiet rapture, that grips many humans also upon their first encounter with a boat.

Rat, undeterred, continued to espouse his love of boats. "In or out of 'em, it doesn't matter. Nothing seems to matter, really, that's the charm of it. Whether you get away, or whether you don't; whether you arrive at your destination or whether you reach somewhere else, or whether you never get anywhere at all, you're always busy, and you never do anything in particular, and when you've done it there's always something else to do . . ."

TIP: If you must have an obsession, boating is better than most.

MILDEW AND MOLD

■ The strangest things eat fiberglass

The tiny organisms known as mildew or mold can eat almost anything anywhere, including your fiberglass boat. These voracious fungi will actually slowly consume the gel coat on the deck of a boat under the right conditions, leaving it pitted and weakened.

Down below, in dark, damp, stagnant air, they will reproduce at an astonishing rate, wreaking havoc on furnishings, sails, plastic fittings, and bulkheads alike. Mildew can even etch the glass in binoculars.

About the only thing mildew can't digest is metal. On anything else, it excretes enzymes that convert complex molecules into soluble compounds capable of passing through its cell walls.

Mildew prefers sub-tropical conditions, but is highly adaptable to colder climates and actually creates its own warmth as it grows, leaving behind that typical musty smell.

Direct sunshine, dry air, and chlorine bleach are the best defenses against mildew. Most commercial mildew removers contain sodium hypochlorite (household bleach). But the best long-term protection is good air circulation throughout the boat to keep ambient humidity low. That means plenty of Dorade boxes, louvered drop boards, and solar-powered vents to keep air passing through and out of the boat.

TIP: Open all locker doors and bilge hatches before you leave the boat for any amount of time, and prop up bunk mattresses so air can circulate underneath.

(See Ventilation)

MOORINGS

■ **Never trust other people's moorings**

A private mooring buoy is always a great temptation to a skipper who is obsessed with the need to find a safe, quiet berth after a hard day's sailing.

The temptation is vastly increased if that enticing buoy also happens to lie among closely anchored yachts where there is no room to allow a decent scope for the anchor line.

But it's a temptation to be resisted.

In the first place, you can't know the condition of the underwater components of the mooring. You also probably won't know what size of boat that mooring was designed to accommodate. You might get away with it if the weather is calm, but if the wind rises and the waves get up you might break the mooring and put yourself in a very dangerous position. Furthermore, where will you go if the owner of the mooring comes back in the middle of the night and kicks you off?

No, steel yourself to another half hour of anxious circling and searching for the anchoring spot that will provoke the fewest fierce glares from those already settled back on their rodes. You'll be a lot safer at anchor.

TIP: In congested anchorages, you can usually get away with a scope of 3 to 1 if you use an all-chain rode.

N

NAUTICAL MILE

■ Call it 2,000 yards and make life easy

The nautical mile is a pleasingly natural measurement, unlike the contrived kilometer and its affected minor offspring. The mariner's mile is simply one-sixtieth of one degree of latitude.

Man's ability to translate degrees of latitude into humble feet and inches has always varied with his ability to measure accurately the surface of the earth, but one degree of latitude has always equaled 60 nautical miles.

For many years, one nautical mile was held to be 6,080 feet, but we now know, thanks to brainier scientists and improved equipment, that it's actually 6,076.1 feet or 2,025.4 yards.

For all practical purposes, the harried navigator on a heaving yacht in bad visibility can take the nautical mile to be 2,000 yards because the extra 25 yards is merely the length of one large yacht. If your navigation is that good, your skipper will have nothing to complain about.

The land mile, used on the Great Lakes, inland rivers, and the Intracoastal Waterway, is still 1,760 yards, as always.

TIP: One-tenth of a nautical mile is a cable—say 200 yards, or a couple of football fields. Since your GPS gives readouts in tenths, you have a ready visual reference for distances in terms of football fields. That's something the metric system can't hope to emulate.

NAVIGATION AIDS

■ Even Red Nuns Carry Odd Green Cans

Navigable channels in U.S. waters are marked with red buoys or daymarks on the starboard side when returning from the open sea. Green buoys or daymarks mark the port side of channels.

To help you when you can't see the color, the buoys and daymarks have distinctive shapes. Red buoys are conical, pointed on top. They're known as nun buoys. Green buoys are flat on top, and are known as can buoys. Red buoys have even numbers and green buoys have odd numbers.

Thus, if you know the color, the shape, or the number of a buoy, you can tell which side of the channel it marks. Here's a memory aid I made up to help me remember: *Even red nuns carry odd green cans.*

But here's the strange thing. *Lighted* buoys do not necessarily conform to the nun or can shapes. In daylight, you can't tell at a distance which side of the channel they're guarding. They mostly look like can buoys with their middles missing.

Daymarks use green squares to mark the port side of the channel (returning from the sea) and red triangles to mark the starboard side.

TIP: Never rely on floating buoys to maintain their exact charted positions. They can shift or even sink and are regularly removed for maintenance.

(See Direction-finding radio; GPS)

NAVIGATION DIFFICULTIES

■ Celestial navigation is neither difficult nor mysterious

In the days before GPS, navigators were much sought-after on deep-sea racing yachts. Many thought themselves to be mighty fine fellows, and strutted around like minor royalty with their charts and sextant boxes tucked under their arms. They maintained a high hedge of mystique around the art of celestial navigation.

Then, in 1950, along came a woman called Mary Blewitt who mowed down their hedges and called their bluff. She wrote a modest 60-page book called *Celestial Navigation for Yachtsmen* that showed everyone how to find their position at sea with no more math than a few simple additions and subtractions.

That book is still in print but I expect sales are down now. There's not much call for celestial navigation when you can get your position in an instant by pushing a button on a GPS receiver.

But if you want to experience the sheer pleasure and profound satisfaction of handling a precision instrument to measure the sun and the stars and plot your position on the chart like centuries of seamen before you, clutch Mary Blewitt to your heart. Then you, too, will be entitled to strut your stuff.

TIP: You can practice taking sights with your sextant at home by shooting the sun in a tray of old engine oil or an artificial horizon.

NAVIGATION LIGHTS

■ **Oil lamps are legal for navigation**

Contrary to what you often hear, kerosene lamps are perfectly legal for running lights and anchor lights. Take no notice of the catalogs that say these lamps are not coast-guard approved. They don't need to be.

Section 11 of Annex 1 of the *International Regulations for Preventing Collisions at Sea* discusses the intensity of non-electric lights. It says: "Non-electric lights shall as far as practicable comply with the minimum intensities, as specified in the Table given in Section 8 of this Annex."

For sailboats less than 12 meters (39 feet 4 inches) in length, this means that your red and green running lights must be visible for one mile. Your masthead light and your sternlight must be visible for 2 miles. Your anchor light must be visible for 2 miles.

Not many of us use kerosene running lights these days, of course, but some of us still have pretty brass kerosene anchor lamps and it's useful to know that a flame from a wick a half-inch wide and a half-inch high can be seen for the legally required 2 miles.

TIP: According to the rules, your anchor light should be visible from all directions and it should be exhibited "where it can best be seen."

NIGHT SAILING

■ **Sailing at night is an act of faith**

Sailing at night can be a wonderful experience, especially in warm southern waters where phosphorescence swirls in your wake and the trade wind sighs gently in the rigging. Brittle stars prick through the velvet canopy of night to guide you on your course and the moon floods the decks with a silver glow.

Sailing at night can also be very frightening, akin to speeding down the freeway blindfolded. Even on the best of nights it's almost impossible to see anything in the water close ahead of you. It's a complete act of faith to presume you have a clear passage.

We all know that containers are washed off freighters regularly. They're floating half-submerged out there, along with deadheads, fishing nets, unlit weather buoys, sleeping whales, and many more things yachts occasionally run into, including each other.

To steer by the compass only, to reef, handle sails, and work on deck in the pitch dark takes practice. Start gradually and gain experience by going out for a couple of hours at twilight. Everything looks different in the dark, even the home port you know so well. Distances are hard to judge and ships' lights are often dangerously confusing.

TIP: Don't start out on an overnight passage unless somebody on board has adequate experience of night sailing.

NON-ESSENTIALS

■ You don't *need* an EPIRB or SSB or GPS or even VHF

There's a lot of equipment you don't *need* on a sailboat, a lot you can get on quite well without.

Basically you need a mast and sails. You need a rudder to steer with and a keel to stop you going sideways. You need ballast to stay upright. You need a cabin with bunks to lie on, a small stove to cook on, and a can opener.

With those things, plus a sextant, and an anchor and line, you can sail around the world, as many others have done before you.

You don't need an engine. You don't need a fridge. You don't need radar, weatherfax, watermakers, hydraulic windlasses, air conditioning, self-tailing winches, electronic instruments, a roller-furling jib, pressure water, stereo sound, single-sideband radio, an EPIRB, a GPS, or even a VHF radio.

If you have the guts and really want to get away from it all and sail around the world, you can do it quite cheaply. The rest of us, chicken-hearted, load our boats with expensive gear whose purpose is to make us feel capable of sailing safely around the world should we ever want to. Which we won't.

TIP: The electronic instrument you'll bless most on a circumnavigation is a depth sounder.

O

OBSESSION

■ **Beware, you may become obsessed with your boat**

My dictionary defines obsession as ". . . a persistent idea, desire, emotion, etc., especially one that cannot be got rid of by reasoning."

People aren't warned when they take up boating that they may become obsessed, but it does happen to a lot of them.

The famous author and sailor, E. B. White was one.

"Waking or sleeping, I dream of boats—usually of rather small boats under a slight press of sail," he wrote in a delightful essay entitled "The Sea and the Wind that Blows" (from *Essays of E. B. White*).

He said that so much of his life had been spent dreaming of small craft that he wondered about the state of his health, for he'd been told that it wasn't a good sign to be always voyaging into unreality, driven by imaginary breezes.

But he concluded: "If a man must be obsessed by something, I suppose a boat is as good as anything, perhaps a bit better than most."

A lot better than most, actually. Obsessing about boats keeps you out of most trouble, as long as you remember to be polite to landlubbers and (especially) as long as you can control the spending urge.

TIP: If obsession cannot be got rid of by reasoning, what's the point of fighting it?

(See Souls)

OSMOSIS

■ **Boat pox is not the end of the world**

Like cancer in humans, osmosis in boats isn't necessarily fatal.

Osmotic blistering of the hull affects about one in four boats. It's caused by the migration of water vapor through the gelcoat into the laminate of glass fibers and polyester resin that we call GRP, or glass-reinforced plastic. The blisters manifest themselves in the outer one-tenth of the GRP.

Blisters come in all sizes, but luckily most of them are fairly small. Consequently, most cures involve nothing more than drilling out the blister site with a conical bit, letting the hole dry out, and then filling it with epoxy and filler.

If you're really unlucky and have a more severe case of blistering, the gelcoat will have to be removed—peeled off by a professional, usually. The hull must be dried thoroughly, often for several months, and the gelcoat must be replaced by coatings of epoxy or vinyl resin.

Bad cases of osmosis are comparatively rare but they are expensive to fix—often amounting to 50 percent of the boat's value or more—so the resale value of an affected boat is low.

TIP: Don't let things get out of hand. Examine the underwater hull every year for osmosis. Catch it quickly, while the blisters are still small and fix it.

OVERHANGS

■ Long overhangs are dangerous at sea

Long overhangs look very elegant on a sailboat. Many racing designs used them at one time or another, boats such as the Thirty Square Meter class, which was limited almost entirely by sail area. Designers searching for the fastest hull for a given sail area came up with slim, narrow boats with minimum underwater surface, and long, long, overhangs to increase speed when the boat heeled. But these were never ocean racing boats.

Long low overhangs are dangerous on open water. They pound badly in a head sea and are easily boarded by large breaking waves. It can be very treacherous to work on a long narrow foredeck awash in heavy weather.

In large quartering seas, such a boat is almost uncontrollable. Each passing swell lifts the long aft overhang and tries to screw the boat around to the broadside-on position. The lever-arm provided by the long overhang means that it takes comparatively little power to spin the boat around. If that happens at speed, the boat will broach and probably capsize, with a good chance of losing the mast. For that reason, most seaboats have only a moderate bow overhang and very little stern overhang.

TIP: Thirty Square Meters and others of that type are wonderful performers in calm water but don't be tempted to take them too far out to sea.

P

PERFORMANCE

■ Your crew won't always be alert

Industrial psychologists assure us that average human performance varies by the time of day. Peak performance hours are usually between 6 a.m. and 11 a.m., after which they taper off until 3 p.m. when a slight surge of improvement takes us up to average levels at about 5 p.m. We perform averagely from then until midnight, when performance drops steeply until 3 a.m.

As a skipper, you need to plan for this, so your crew is always able to manage the boat properly.

Long ocean trips bring their own complications, of course. Crews get bored and inattentive. They doze off. They get seasick. Do what you can to keep them alert. Set watches and insist that they go below to sleep by day in their off-watches, even if just to rest on a bunk.

They'll only give of their best if they're well fed, well rested, warm, and dry. So good, hot food and foulweather gear are also important. They'll also think and work better if you involve them in the business of sailing and navigation. Keep them interested.

TIP: On short trips there's no time for the crew to become accustomed to regular night watches. So make the watches as short as possible between midnight and 4 a.m.

(See Watchkeeping)

PETS

■ **The only pet for a boat is a parrot. Maybe**

Dogs and cats are so much a part of some families that they have to be taken sailing with their owners.

But dogs can be a considerable nuisance. They need to be ferried ashore every day, or trained to do their doggy business on mats that can be shaken overboard, and they can't stop themselves barking at every passing seagull.

I knew a young couple in San Diego whose anchored 28-foot sloop was carefully avoided by anyone in a dinghy. Their pet was a large, excitable, and over-friendly German shepherd who would enthusiastically launch himself off the sloop into any dinghy that passed close enough, often with disastrous results.

Cats can be wonderful companions on a boat. They're clean, compact, less demanding, and sleep 16 hours a day. I met one called Pepe who, during a circumnavigation on a 40-footer, had been taught to use the head. He was not only talented but lucky. The more usual fate of cats is to fall overboard and drown.

A parrot is surely the pet most closely associated with sailors.

Parrots live a long time, eat little food, and can swear at people you don't like. But they demand attention and can get quite cantankerous when ignored.

TIP: If you're going abroad, check on other countries' restrictions on pets.

PLANKTON

■ You can survive in a life raft without food and water

People who take to life rafts in mid-ocean often die prematurely because they see no hope of survival. Despair and hopelessness take over when they're forced to wait passively for rescue in a raft that's simply drifting.

Psychologically, your chances of survival are much greater if you can guide the raft toward safety, no matter how far away. The ability to sail and steer a raft makes even the most desperate situation bearable.

Physically, you can survive if you know about plankton, the micro-organisms that come to the surface on dark nights. Dr. Alain Bombard, a French physician, drifted across the Atlantic without food or water in 1952 in a rubber life raft called L'HÉRÉTIQUE to prove that point. He dragged a fine net behind the raft and survived on the fish and plankton he caught.

If you can trawl a shirt or some makeshift net through the water at one or two knots, you'll end up with a nourishing soup of plankton. Certain fish juices contain high percentages of fresh water and, of course, your raft will catch passing showers of rain.

TIP: In calm water after heavy rainfall, the top inch or so of the ocean is mostly fresh water floating on top of salt water. Scoop it into your raft.

(See Drinking seawater; Freshwater supplies; Water)

POLLUTION

■ Many sailors break the pollution laws

Scientists have yet to prove conclusively that human waste is detrimental to sea creatures. Experiments conducted by prestigious institutes of marine biology have shown that while some creatures move away from underwater sewage outlets, others settle in to take their places. Sewage is, after all, fertilizer.

Many people therefore question the logic of taking human waste, mixing it with biocidal chemicals, and then returning the contaminated sewage to the ocean. For millions of years, sea creatures have swum in their untreated excreta. Granted, the vast and increasing number of humans means their waste is reaching the oceans in record amounts, but think for one moment of the sheer volume of waste excreted by just one blue whale.

There's no doubt that most boaters break the pollution laws occasionally, either by peeing overboard or dumping a holding tank within three miles of the shore, because no pump-out facilities are handy.

Such things happen. And who can say the sea has been hurt? Waste is mostly sterile. What pathogens do exist usually succumb quickly to salt and sunlight.

No one with a conscience would pollute a marina or an enclosed bay, but in open water where the currents run, where's the harm?

TIP: All boats operating in U.S. waters with permanently installed toilets must have a holding tank.

PRICES

■ You can sail around the world in a boat costing less than a used car

Boatbuilders in the early days of fiberglass could never have imagined how long their products would last. After 15 or 20 years, a boatbuilder could rely on a wooden boat to do the decent thing and rot away into oblivion. But today, 40- or 50-year-old fiberglass boats are still going strong and depressing sales of new boats.

Consequently, there are many bargains to be found among old-fashioned but sound sailboats capable of sailing around the world. Like aging film stars caught off-guard, they may look slightly seedy and down at heel in the glare of the spotlight, but after a good paint job and some body work they'll be as good as ever.

If you're young and not too concerned with creature comfort, you can even find old fiberglass boats, capable of crossing oceans, that bear price tags with figures lower than those of many used cars. They naturally won't offer the comfort and style of newer designs, but the sea doesn't care about that. The sea respects only seaworthiness, and the design aspects of seaworthiness don't change as the demands of modern styling and accommodations do.

TIP: Size is not the main arbiter of seaworthiness. Boats of 20 feet and up regularly cross oceans. The smaller and simpler the boat, the less money you'll need to make your dreams come true.

(See Boat choice)

PRIVACY

∎ On a long trip, privacy is greatly important

Ordinary, likeable people can become very crabby when they're locked up in the close confines of a yacht with several others for any length of time.

This is a serious business for any skipper to deal with because privacy on a small yacht is about as attainable as silence on a school bus.

On land, we unconsciously preserve our personal spaces but when we're sailing we have to put up with constant invasions of our privacy for long periods by people we may not even like.

Nevertheless, the skipper must try to ensure that every crewmember has at least a token amount of space which is his or hers alone, and that this fact is understood by everybody. A curtained-off pilot berth, separated from the rest of the thundering herd, is the ultimate fantasy, but rarely available. Even a bunk of your own may not be possible if other crewmembers have to sit on it, too.

In this case, a personal drawer or small private locker must suffice as a place where you can hide your last beer or bar of chocolate from the prying eyes and thieving fingers of the hoi polloi.

TIP: Psychologists recommend that you never sail with more crew than there are individual bunks for.

PROPELLERS

■ **Even to designers, propellers are a mystery**

Ever since the first ship's propellers evolved about 150 years ago, designers have been trying to unravel their mysteries. New York naval architect Dave Gerr says in his book, *The Nature of Boats*, that there are "more theories of propeller behavior and performance than you could fit on a shelf full of books—a sure sign we don't fully understand them."

Little wonder, then, that sailboaters fretting about the performance of their craft under power often wonder if they have a propeller of the right diameter and pitch.

Trial and error is the way most new boats are mated with their propellers. The ideal propeller will allow the engine to reach the manufacturer's top-rated revolutions per minute (and therefore full power) with the throttle opened fully. And at this stage, your boat should be achieving full hull speed.

If your engine starts to lug or emit black smoke before it reaches top-rated revs, it can't develop full power and the engine will be overloaded at *all* speeds. Try reducing the propeller pitch. If your engine reaches top revs too easily, before your boat reaches hull speed, try increasing the pitch.

TIP: A propeller shop can alter the pitch of most auxiliary yacht propellers for a fraction of the cost of a new propeller.

R

RACING

■ Experience of racing makes a better cruiser

Cruisers who insist they don't care about speed are really saying they don't care about efficiency. The efficiency of the sails creates power, and power is what drives the boat forward. It's not only satisfying to be able to develop more power. It could save your life if you have to beat off a lee shore in heavy weather.

Nothing makes a sailor more aware of how sails develop power than racing. When an identical boat starts pulling away from you, or pointing higher, you have to wonder what's happening, and why.

Racing teaches you how the sails should look in different strengths of wind, when they are working, when they are stalled, and how they should be trimmed for a beat or a reach. And, in a race, you can see the results immediately. All these adjustments come so naturally after a little practice that they become second nature; you don't have to think about them.

When you're cruising, it's very satisfying to know that you're getting the most out of the wind, that you're not wasting what nature is providing so freely.

TIP: The truly laid-back cruiser need feel no compunction for not retrimming the sails after every little change in the wind's strength or direction. That's not the crime. The crime is not knowing how, when it's necessary.

(See Relative speeds, Speed)

RADAR

■ Radar pictures don't look anything like the real thing

Radar installations have become quite common on small yachts, especially along the foggier areas of our coastline, but I have serious doubts about how efficient they are.

Professional radar operators go to radar school to learn how best to use their units, and how to interpret what shows on the screens when they're being used properly.

My skepticism arises from the fact that most amateurs don't take the time to learn the intricacies of radar operation. They don't understand what they might be *missing*, in addition to what they're *seeing*. And comparatively few are even qualified to interpret what they're seeing, particularly when the weather is bad and wave clutter is strong.

Radar is undoubtedly a wonderful safety feature if it's used correctly, but it must be used with great circumspection. Even expert radar operators such as those on the passenger liners ANDREA DORIA and STOCKHOLM, which collided off the U.S. coast, have made colossal mistakes in interpretation. Each had the other in plain view on radar.

TIP: It's very difficult for radar to detect a small change in the course of an approaching vessel. If you want to make sure of being noticed on the other vessel's radar, make a course change of at least 60 degrees.

(See Fog; Radar reflectors)

RADAR REFLECTORS

■ **Never presume another ship can "see" you**

Small yachts are notoriously difficult for large ships to detect on their radar screens. Radar's high-frequency radio waves must be reflected back to the transmitter to be "seen," so the best targets are those composed of dense material, such as rock or metal, and those having large flat surfaces.

Wooden boats present poor targets, and fiberglass boats are not much better, because very little of the original radar transmission bounces back to the source. Even metal targets such as aluminum masts or booms are poor targets because their round sections scatter the return signal in many directions, so that very little of the original power arrives back at the transmitter.

To ensure that more of the signal is returned, we use radar reflectors made of metal and cunningly fashioned so that a radar transmission entering from any angle will be returned along a reciprocal path at full strength.

The higher you place your reflector, the farther away it will be detected but, remember, it's still a very small target compared with a steel ship, and your little blip might not attract much attention on another vessel's radar screen.

TIP: The bigger your reflector, the better, even by inches. If you double the size of a reflector, its effectiveness increases an astonishing 16 times.

(See Avoiding collisions; Fog; Radar)

RAIN

■ Sailing in the rain is miserable

Years ago I raced deepsea with a skipper who loved rain. He used to roar at it and laugh loudly with his face upturned to the heavens. He would punch rain drops with clenched fists, and wriggle with delight as icy streams trickled down his back. I thought then that he was abnormal, and I still do. Normal people like me think it's miserable to sail in the rain, especially cold rain.

But now and then most of us *have* to sail in the rain because the great majority of sailboats have open cockpits at the aft end of the boat. From there you can see the sails and feel the strength and direction of the wind, but you don't get much protection from the weather.

To make the best of a bad thing, you need good foulweather gear. Most of today's waterproof jackets come with attached hoods but many people don't like hoods because they tend to stand still while you turn your head, thus restricting your line of sight to dead ahead.

The best rain headgear in my opinion is the tried and tested fisherman's sou'wester, with a thin woolen watch cap underneath.

TIP: If you wear glasses and need a peak to keep off rain, wear a baseball cap under your hood.

(*See Drinking seawater; Freshwater supplies; Water*)

REEFING

■ It's O.K. to reef early

One of the greatest thrills in sailing is the feeling of being fully in control of a boat in heavy weather. It's wonderfully satisfying and very reassuring when a boat fighting heavy winds and seas will respond quickly and surely to the lightest touch on the helm.

To reach this much-desired state of balance, you must reduce sail area by reefing and/or changing large sails for smaller ones. It's not smart to struggle on with the boat lying over on her ear and the tiller up under your chin. In fact, it's downright dangerous.

Reef as soon as the thought occurs to you. The later you leave it, the more difficult it is to tame the flapping canvas and haul the mainsail clew out to make an efficient flat shape. You'll often hear that reefing will make you go faster but that's not necessarily true. You'll notice that round-the-buoys racers rarely reef, no matter what the weather.

Ocean racers reef, though, because crew fatigue and efficiency is more of a concern over long periods than a slight loss in speed, and having the boat under tight control is a great morale builder.

TIP: On most boats, if you're short-handed it's much easier to reef the mainsail if you first heave to, preferably on the starboard tack.

(See Wind strength)

RELATIVE SPEEDS

■ All boats are relatively slow

Newcomers to sailing must find it hard to hide their smirks when they hear old salts referring to fast boats and slow boats. In truth, all sailboats are slow in comparison with other forms of transport.

The very fastest sailboats have emerged in the past few years. In March, 2001, the record-breaking 110-foot catamaran CLUB MED took 62 days to circumnavigate the earth. She covered 26,500 miles at an average speed of 18.2 knots. One day she sailed 650 nautical miles— a 24-hour average of 27 knots.

But she was a highly specialized boat. Most small sailboats cross oceans at a rate of about 120 miles every 24 hours, a distance that takes only two hours in a family car.

Luckily, one of the great charms of sailing is that speed, time, and distance lose the importance we grant them on land. They mingle, dissolve, and gel into a form of joy unknown to landlubbers. Yes, sailing is slow, but that only means its delights last longer.

TIP: Speed in a sailboat is often obtained at the expense of sturdiness, seaworthiness, accommodations, and carrying capacity.

(See Lies; Racing, Seaworthiness, Speed)

RENAMING A BOAT

■ **It's OK to rename your boat if you know how**

One thing you learn very quickly is that boat names are very personal. Very few new owners are happy with the name the previous owner gave the boat. What often stops them from changing the name is the threat of the bad luck that many people believe will follow.

Sailors are among the most superstitious groups on earth because they know they need all the luck they can get out there and there's no point in offending the gods unnecessarily.

But there is a way to sidestep this dilemma. Years ago I wrote a denaming ceremony, which cleanses the boat of the old name, thus preparing it for a brand-new christening with the new name.

I have changed the names of boats this way several times. Hundreds of other owners have also used my denaming ceremony with great success. You'll find the full ceremony and instructions here in the appendix of useful tables and formulas.

TIP: If you choose champagne for the part of the ceremony known as the libation, buy as good a bottle as you can reasonably afford. The gods of the wind and sea despise meanness.

(See Luck)

REPAINTING

■ **Even an amateur can do a professional paint job**

In the bad old days, when boats were made of wood, hulls were repainted regularly. Most owners did this work themselves, so the results were often less than perfect. Nobody cared much, though. If you couldn't pick out the runs and old scratches from 50 feet away, the job was considered plenty good enough.

That happy state of affairs ended when fiberglass boats were invented. Their hulls had the mirror finish of Dresden china. The seductive promise was that they would never need repainting and it was almost true. But after a good few years in the sun, gel coats start to oxidize. That dullness, combined with the inevitable scuffs and scratches of everyday use, dictates paint jobs for the topsides.

The best paint for this job is a twin-pack polyurethane. It's tougher than the original gel coat but it has a reputation for being tricky to apply. Amateurs are now wary because on these ultra-smooth hulls a good job looks wonderful but all mistakes are magnified. In fact, though, amateurs can roll-and-tip this paint with complete success. All it takes is the courage to start and the knowledge that if you foul it up, you can sand it down and start again.

TIP: Build your skills by first painting a dinghy or your boat's transom.

RESPONSIBILITY

■ **If you're in charge, delegate responsibility**

Dr. Michael Stadler says in *The Psychology of Sailing*: "In many respects the situation at sea does not differ in principle from the situation in a prison or cloister. Sociologists have described such living conditions as 'total institutions.'" That means all activities

are carried out in the same living space, with the same objective, under one authority.

As the skipper of a boat at sea, you are that authority—and thus the target of every gripe and resentment. As skipper, the law requires that you accept full responsibility for what happens on your boat, but you shouldn't keep to yourself all the difficult tasks that require a high degree of skill, such as steering in bad weather, navigation, docking maneuvers, sail changes, and so on.

It's smarter, for your good and theirs, to teach and delegate. Offer your crew the opportunity to learn and develop their own skills. Give them responsibility in the day-to-day running of the ship. In this way, you'll instill a sense of team spirit and the satisfying feeling that they're making valuable contributions to the welfare of the group. And (not coincidentally) it also keeps them too busy to think about mutiny.

TIP: The wise skipper checks on the crew's work without their being aware of it, and intervenes only if need be.

(See Who's in charge?)

RIGGING

■ Find out what toggles are and use them

The wires holding up your mast are subject to dangerous metal fatigue where they join the mast and the hull. The problem is vibration, or repeated cycling and flexing. Most metal, if you repeatedly work it back and forth, will crack and break.

In the early days of Comet jet airliners, the wings of planes actually broke off at the roots because the effect of metal fatigue through flexing was not properly understood.

A similar thing can happen to your stays and shrouds if they're not properly attached. While the result may not be as catastrophic, it's inconvenient, to say the least, to have your mast fall down.

Although your wire rigging appears to be very firmly attached at either end, it actually flexes slightly under certain circumstances. Even at the dock, or at anchor, the wires will jiggle back and forth when the wind speed is right. Vibrations from the engine have the same effect. Although this flexing is not visually dramatic its effects are cumulative.

The answer is to use small universal joints, known as toggles, at the mast tang and hull chainplates, so that the wire is free to move in *all* directions without being bent.

TIP: Some turnbuckles have toggles built in, but many do not. Be sure to check yours.

RIGHT OF WAY

■ **Sailboats don't always have the right of way over powerboats**

When you're a newcomer to sailing, one of the first rules you learn is that power gives way to sail. But that's not the whole story. There are some occasions when sail must give way to power.

The rules say that a sailing vessel shall keep out of the way of a vessel not under command, a vessel restricted in her ability to maneuver, and a vessel engaged in fishing.

In addition there are three overriding rules. Rule 9 says a sailboat shall not impede the passage of a vessel that can safely navigate only within a narrow channel or fairway. Rule 10 is implemented where there are traffic separation schemes. It states that a sailing vessel shall not impede the safe passage of a power-driven vessel following a traffic lane.

And the final overriding rule, Rule 13, says quite simply that any vessel overtaking another shall keep out of the way of the vessel being overtaken. So if you in your sailboat are overtaking a powerboat, you must keep clear of her.

TIP: Note that the only fishing vessel a sailboat must give way to is one that cannot maneuver because of the gear she has overboard. You don't have to cede way to fishing boats trailing only lines and lures.

(See Avoiding collisions)

RIGS

■ There is no "best" rig

Most sailboats up to about 30 feet in length are sloops, and most are Bermudan-rigged. Very few are gaff-rigged these days, though that low, sturdy, and attractive rig still makes a good deal of sense for dedicated ocean voyagers.

From 30 feet upward, there are choices to be made between cutters, yawls, ketches, and schooners. No matter what their supporters say, none of these is "better" than the others. They all have their good points and bad points. The best rig is simply the one that most efficiently does the job required of it.

The sloop is the simplest rig, and usually the most efficient and closewinded. It's nimble and ideal for racing boats and fast cruisers. When the one large headsail becomes a burden, the rig can be split into three sails to ease handling. Yawls are few these days (the tiny mizzensail was beneficial under an old racing rule) but ketches are popular because you can simply douse individual sails instead of reefing. Cutters conveniently split the headsail area, and schooners spread the canvas farther fore and aft for better balance, but both give up some weatherliness compared with the sloop.

TIP: Where there's a choice, always go for the simplest rig you can safely handle singlehanded, or with the minimum crew.

(See Tradewind sailing)

RUNNING LIGHTS

■ Your lights may be invisible at sea

Don't ever rely on your navigation lights being seen by a large ship at sea. Even if you have the right of way, it's better that you take avoiding action because sailboat lights are notoriously difficult to see and interpret.

That's not surprising, considering the problems: they're not far above the sea's surface; they're not very bright; they're often heeled over at odd angles; and they may be blanketed, steadily or occasionally, by spray, sails, or spars.

The best place for port and starboard lights is atop the bow pulpit where they're most protected from spray. They should be the brightest lights your electrical power system can manage because colored glass absorbs 85 to 90 percent of the light from the bulb.

It takes a 24-watt bulb to be visible through red or green plastic at a little over a mile in the most favorable weather conditions. That range is extended to about three miles if the bulb is shining through clear glass or plastic.

TIP: A tricolor light at the masthead uses only one bulb for the port, starboard, and stern lights and is the most economical for a boat under sail alone. It cannot be used under power, however, because the masthead light must be higher than the sidelights.

(See Avoiding collisions)

RUNNING RIGGING

■ You need only three kinds of rope

Unless you're a high-tech racer you can forget about all those exotic, high-modulus, expensive lines such as Kevlar, Technora, Vectran, Zylon, and even the more common Spectra.

All you really need for the great majority of sailboats is nylon, polyester, and polypropylene. All of these shed water, resist rot, and dry quickly. They are resilient and very strong. For instance, the conservative breaking strength of half-inch-diameter nylon line is 5,000 pounds.

Nylon has the ability to stretch and absorb shock loads slowly, so it's ideal for anchor rodes and dock lines.

Polyester, known in the United States by its trademark name, Dacron, stretches very little and is thus suitable for sheets and halyards.

Three-strand nylon and Dacron are easy to splice. Lines with braided covers are slightly stronger and better protected, but harder to splice.

Polypropylene is not as strong as the other two and it doesn't retain knots well. But it's cheaper and has a unique attribute: unlike nylon and Dacron, it floats. Many dinghy painters are therefore made of polypropylene on the theory that it will keep the line out of the boat's propeller. That theory, unfortunately, isn't always supported by practice.

TIP: All three are slowly degraded by sunlight, polypropylene the quickest, so it pays to protect them as much as possible.

(See Splicing)

S

SAFETY HARNESSES

■ Be aware that safety equipment can kill you

It's hard to know how many sailors' lives have been saved by safety harnesses. No disinterested authority seems to keep the relevant statistics. But I know for a fact that a harness killed one sailor and would have killed another had his boat not run aground.

The fatality occurred in a storm off the South African coast when a racing fleet was overwhelmed by a sudden southwesterly "buster." A fairly beamy 26-foot sloop was capsized by a large wave and stayed upside down a long time. One of her cockpit crew couldn't release the tether of his safety harness and drowned before she righted herself.

Yukio Hasebe, a singlehanded Japanese circumnavigator, almost drowned when he fell off his 30-foot sloop and was dragged alongside the hull. He couldn't pull himself aboard. The boat sped on, steered by her windvane, for hours while Hasebe fought for breath and was badly scraped by barnacles. He was almost exhausted when the boat grounded on a reef off Australia. He lost the boat but saved his life.

Lessons: make sure you can detach your tether at your breast, even under strain; and think hard about how to get back aboard if you go over the side.

TIP: Whenever you can, use a tether short enough to *prevent* your falling overboard.

(See Crew overboard)

SAIL MATERIALS

■ **You don't need fancy multi-ply sails unless you're racing**

In Sven Donaldson's excellent book *Understanding the New Sailing Technology* the author points out that the majority of today's sails are still being made from woven sailcloths that are, at best, only marginally improved over the materials in use during the 1970s.

Although Donaldson's book was published in 1990, his statement still holds. Although the new technology of laminated sails is going strong, comparatively few sailboats are using sails of Spectra, Kevlar, Mylar and other exotic materials because of their higher cost and reduced life.

Dedicated racing boats are the major customers for high-tech sails, of course, because of their greater efficiency. But if you don't mind dropping behind by a few seconds a mile, cheaper nylon and polyester (Dacron) sails will do just fine, accept more knocks, and last longer.

While improvements are being made all the time to the fibers, weave, design, and construction of "ordinary" sails, especially with the help of computers, it's likely that laminated sails and glued panels will point the way to the future for all sailboats.

But don't rush things. The future isn't here yet. Sailors are ultra-conservative, and for very good reasons.

TIP: One-design racing has shown that laminated sails aren't consistently faster than *new* sails made from firm-finished Dacron sailcloth.

(See Spinnakers)

SAILING ON FRIDAY

■ **It's safe to sail on Friday if you take this precaution**

Before the birth of Christ, Friday was a good day to sail on. After all, the day was named after the Norse goddess Frigg, the wife of Odin, the most powerful of all gods. She was the goddess of love and fertility, but early Christians contended that she was a witch. After that abrupt about-face, it was considered bad luck to sail on the witch's day.

To this day, highly superstitious sailors all over the world will have nothing to do with sailing on Friday, despite overwhelming evidence that the vast majority of ships sailing on Fridays arrive at their destinations unscathed.

There is a precaution you can take, however, if you simply must set sail on Friday. The trick is to start your voyage on Wednesday or Thursday. Cast off, sail a couple of miles on your intended course, and then turn back to attend to some small problem that seems to have arisen. Perhaps you forgot to top off the water tanks. Perhaps the cheese has gone moldy, or a shackle has lost its pin.

Then, when Friday comes, you can sail again in earnest because you are now *continuing* the earlier voyage, not starting a new one.

TIP: If you're wise, you won't scoff outright at old maritime superstitions. The sea has not yet unfolded all its mysteries.

SAILING SKILL

■ **If you can sail a 10-foot dinghy, you can sail anything**

Nothing beats a small dinghy when you want to learn how to sail. There are no distractions to come between you and the starkest principles of handling a vessel under sail.

The basic elements of beating, coming about, running, and jibing are common to all sailboats, but when you put the helm down in a small dinghy, the results are immediately apparent. You don't have to wonder what to expect. In a few moments, you have learned the principle of getting enough way on the ship to enable her to tack through the eye of the wind, and the art of balancing her helm with the sails.

There's practically nothing you can do on a large vessel that you can't do in a dinghy, including backing the jib to heave to. In fact, a dinghy teaches you skills you'll probably never need on a larger boat, such as sailing backward, which is quite easy in a dinghy, and the art of steering in reverse without letting the rudder slam over and damage itself.

On bigger boats, exactly the same principles apply. The only difference is that everything happens more slowly, and cause doesn't seem as connected to effect.

TIP: Most experts agree that sailing should be taught on boats of 25 feet or less.

(*See Learning to sail*)

SALVAGE

■ **You have to save lives at sea, but not vessels**

If you come across a boat in trouble, maritime law says you have to try to save the lives of its crew. But there is nothing to compel you to save the vessel.

If, however, you decide to drag her off the rocks, or put out the fire, or pump her bilges and tow her to a safe harbor, you may qualify for a reward.

Firstly, the boat must have been in grave danger of being lost or badly damaged. Secondly, you must have *volunteered* your help. Thirdly, you must have risked your life or your property in your bid to aid the stricken boat. And fourthly (and a little unfairly I've always thought) your efforts must be successful. You'll get nothing if you can't manage to deliver what's left of her to a safe harbor, even if you've worked on her for days.

How much can you claim for salvage? Admiralty Court awards are usually based on how much your efforts contributed to saving the boat. To qualify at all, your efforts must have been "substantial," compared with any other help the vessel might have received.

TIP: Take no notice of the old fairy tale that handing your towline to another boat entitles you to claim salvage. It's not automatic.

SCULLING

■ This useful trick will get you lots of attention

If you ever lose or break an oar while you're rowing in a dinghy you'll be glad you learned to scull. With one oar over the stern you can scull your way to safety slowly but surely.

It's a useful skill to learn because, although it's not as fast as regular rowing, it's smooth and powerful. Once when my 27-foot sailboat's engine died, I towed her into a crowded marina by sculling from the dinghy.

The advantage of sculling is that the oar never leaves the water, so its power is applied smoothly and steadily without breaks. When you try to tow a heavy boat from a rowboat with two oars, the dinghy wastes a lot of your energy by jerking and snatching at the painter.

Sculling is also a spectator sport. People always stop to stare at someone sculling, as if it were the enactment of an ancient and long-forgotten art.

You can scull over the stern with an ordinary rowlock, but it's easier to use a dedicated sculling notch. That notch is an egg-shaped cutout atop the transom, about $1\frac{7}{8}$ inches wide and $2\frac{1}{2}$

inches deep, but narrowing at the top. It can be offset from the center as convenient.

TIP: The easiest dinghies to scull are heavy, narrow, and deep.

SEA MONSTERS

■ **Don't scoff. Sea monsters really do exist**

Anyone who goes to sea knows that you should be more afraid of tentacles than jaws. Sharks are well known and understood. They're a visible threat with known consequences. It's the mysterious giant squid that puts the fear of God into honest seafarers.

David Attenborough, the famous adventurer and biologist, says in *Life on Earth*: "Squids grow to an immense size. In 1933, in New Zealand, one was recorded that was 21 meters (69 feet) long, with eyes 40 centimeters (nearly 16 inches) across, the largest known eyes in the animal kingdom."

Even so, we haven't yet discovered the biggest squids because they are extremely intelligent and difficult to catch, Attenborough says. He concludes that it's by no means impossible that the kraken and other legendary sea monsters that are said to be able to rise from the deep and wrap ships in their tentacles, really do exist.

TIP: If you catch a squid on a trailing line, take care. Michael Greenwald, an author and yachtsman, caught one of about 30 pounds in mid-Atlantic that squirted him in the face with a powerful acid and tried to drag him overboard. By the time he had struggled free, and washed his face, the acid had eaten holes in his woolen sweater.

SEACOCKS

■ Watch out for bad seacocks

There are usually several holes in a boat's hull through which fluids pass in or out. For obvious reasons, every one of those holes should have a sturdy shut-off valve attached to it. For equally obvious reasons, those valves, which we call seacocks, should be solid, long-lasting, and reliable. Unfortunately, good seacocks are expensive, so some boatbuilders make do with cheaper substitutes.

Replacing bad seacocks is a costly business, so if you're buying a boat be sure to check them carefully. The three types of approved seacocks for small boats are:

The traditional tapered-plug type;

The T-bar type with a swelling plug; and

The ball-valve type with a bronze body and a ball turning in a Teflon seal.

They should all be made of marine-grade bronze. Beware of cheap brass. Beware, also, of any type of screw-down gate valve, because you can't tell if they're properly closed or merely screwed down onto a piece of unyielding debris.

All seacocks should be tightly screwed onto the through-hull fittings that line the holes in the hull, and their flanges and backing plates should be tightly bolted through the hull.

TIP: Corrosion-proof seacocks made of glass-reinforced nylon, known as Marelon, are also widely used but as yet do not have the proven track record of solid bronze-bodied seacocks.

SEAKINDLINESS

■ Don't expect comfort in a small boat at sea

You shouldn't expect any sailboat under 40 feet to provide much comfort in a choppy sea. The very qualities necessary to ensure

survival, such as maximum buoyancy and fast reaction to changing water levels, result in the kind of quick, jerky motion that causes seasickness and difficulty in moving about—sometimes even difficulty in staying put.

That said, some designs are kinder to humans than others. The well-known naval architect Ted Brewer, who invented a formula for a "comfort ratio," says that quickness of motion, or "corkiness," is determined mainly by two factors: the beam of the hull and the area of the waterline.

What this translates to is that it's more comfortable to sail in a boat that's comparatively narrower, deeper, and heavier than another of the same length.

Most classic full-keel designs fulfill those requirements. They're slightly slower to react to waves and swells because of their increased inertia. They're less likely to be capsized by a breaking wave and it's safer to work on the deck of such a boat, though they may be wetter. Comfort naturally increases with size, but it increases more quickly with displacement than with length.

TIP: At any given length, comfort is gained at the expense of some other desirable qualities, most often speed, weatherliness, and accommodations.

(See Inertia; Seaworthiness)

SEASICKNESS

■ Find the right drug *before* you get seasick

Seasickness appears to be caused by a sensory conflict between the eyes and the balance system of the inner ear. It happens, for example, when you're down below in choppy seas, and the eyes, watching the interior of the cabin, detect no motion. Your inner ear, however, *feels* the rising, sinking, and heeling movements of the boat and insists there *is* motion. Hence the conflict. But why the nausea? Nobody knows.

We cannot entirely prevent seasickness. If conditions are violent, almost everyone will suffer unless they have taken drugs to ward it off.

If you're planning a long trip, don't wait until you're feeling sick to try a new drug. Consult your doctor well in advance and experiment with some compatible drugs at home to discover whether you suffer from side effects such as drowsiness, dry mouth, blurred vision, and headaches.

Incidentally, it takes time for a drug to begin to act. Some manufacturers recommend you take their drugs 12 hours before sailing, or the night before departure.

TIP: One of the most effective drugs is Scopolamine, available in a small adhesive patch worn behind the ear, and good for three days.

SEAWORTHINESS

■ Bigger boats aren't necessarily more seaworthy

While it's certainly true that a good big boat is more seaworthy than a good small boat, you can't judge seaworthiness by size alone. The renowned naval architect Howard I. Chapelle defined seaworthiness as "basically the ability of a boat to live in heavy weather without swamping, capsizing, breaking up, or being heavily damaged while under way." By that token, many small sailboats such as John Guzzwell's 21-foot circumnavigator, TREKKA, have proved themselves extremely seaworthy.

An adequate number of crew with seagoing experience is worth more than intrinsic seaworthiness in a boat of any size. Indeed, any number of "unsuitable" boats have made memorable voyages in the hands of skilled sailors, and some very seaworthy boats have come croppers under inexperienced skippers.

The factors more affected by size are speed and creature comfort. Small boats are naturally slower than big ones, which might be able to move quickly out of the path of a storm. In this way, size might add to seaworthiness. And small boats, especially those of light displacement, become increasingly uncomfortable with diminishing size.

TIP: The veteran British sailor Eric Hiscock held that the larger the vessel the better for ocean voyaging, *provided her management is within the capabilities of her crew and within their financial scope.* He twice circumnavigated in a 30-footer.

(See Keel design; Seakindliness; Speed)

SEAWORTHY STERNS

■ A transom stern is just as seaworthy as a double-ender

Much has been made, and continues to be made, of the seaworthiness of pointed sterns, compared with transom or counter sterns. North Sea lifeboats and pilot boats are famous for having sterns shaped very much like their bows. Their ability to part seas easily have made double-enders, such as the Colin Archer type, and canoe-sterns, such as the modern Pacific Seacraft designs of California designer William Crealock, much admired for their running ability in heavy conditions.

But there is no evidence whatsoever to suggest that such sterns are more seaworthy than others. In fact, they may be less so, since the lack of reserve buoyancy aft leaves them more prone to pooping. Furthermore, because of the very rounded buttocks they produce, lifeboat sterns almost invariably produce slow boats. Canoe sterns mostly avoid this problem.

The distinguished North American naval architect Ted Brewer points out in his book *Understanding Boat Design* that the main advantage of pointed sterns was specific to their function as work-boats. "There was no transom corner to be smashed in when the pilot boat pulled away from a freighter in a rough sea, or to foul the net of a fishing boat," he says.

TIP: When considering the seaworthiness of a boat, discount any suggestion that transoms or counters are less able than pointed sterns.

(See Seaworthiness)

SELLING

■ You don't need a broker to sell your boat

The smaller the boat, the less likely you are to need a yacht broker to help you sell her. In fact, brokers aren't much interested in boats under about 27 feet because their reward is usually 10 percent of the selling price, and that doesn't come to much on small boats, which take just as much time and effort to sell as do bigger boats.

You can advertise the boat yourself and do the paperwork. If she's documented, download and print the official Bill of Sale from the U.S. Coast Guard website. Fill it in and have it notarized. For State-numbered boats, simply sign the title document.

Meanwhile, strip the boat of all your stuff. Buyers want to imagine their stuff there. Have the boat professionally cleaned. It's worth it. Prepare a simple brochure that lists everything aboard in minute detail. Assemble a file containing all the manuals, warranties, licenses, and paperwork you have.

Here's what puts buyers off: Dirt, rust stains, wood rot, frayed lines, mildew, musty smells, diesel or gas smells, torn upholstery, dirty bilges, peeling varnish, an engine that won't start, dirty fenders, and badly worn sails.

TIP: Probably nothing impresses a knowledgeable buyer more than newly painted, clean, and absolutely dry bilges.

SIGNAL MIRRORS

■ **How the sun's reflection can save your life**

Nothing arouses our curiosity quicker than a bright light flashing insistently on the far horizon. That's why a signal mirror is one of the best safety devices a boat can carry.

John Butler, a former Coast Guard search-and-rescue pilot, says he and his crew have seen mirror signals from 43 miles away and Coast Guard records mention that rescue aircraft have seen them from as much as 100 miles distant.

Almost any highly reflective flat surface can be used in an emergency. The shiny side of a compact disk works well. Even a credit card can work. In 1991, four castaways used a credit card to attract attention when they were drifting 100 miles out in the Gulf Stream, where their plane crash landed.

There must be sunshine, of course, and you have to aim the sun's reflection by extending your arm, holding up your fingers in a V that embraces the target, and shooting through the V.

But the best reflector is a dedicated glass signaling mirror with a central device about an inch in diameter that produces a fireball or bright spot for precision aiming.

TIP: While there are several excellent glass and plastic mirrors on the market, the standard to beat is still the old standard GI-issue 3-inch by 5-inch glass mirror.

SIMPLE SOLUTIONS

■ Boat equipment doesn't need to be so complicated

We sailors are a strange lot. We love bright and shiny things, especially bright and shiny things with batteries (and digital cameras built in).

We trust stainless steel, fiberglass, and chrome. We mistrust rope and wood. We love electronics. We love fridges, microwaves, hot showers, ovens, and even electric heads that save us the effort of waggling the handle for a few moments. In short, we took one of the simplest forms of transport in the world and made it complicated.

Many of the fittings and systems aboard our boats are there purely for our creature comfort and have nothing to do with their suitability for sailing, especially long-distance cruising.

We don't need mainsail flaking systems, full-length battens, and batten cars. We don't need fancy, expensive air blocks that offer no great advantage, except to the manufacturer's profits. We don't need self-tailing winches if we're prepared to luff up for a couple of moments, and there's no need for many of the complicated chrome and stainless fittings we dote on if there's a piece of line handy. But we buy all these things anyway. Let's face it—we've lost the ability or will to think simply.

TIP: Three thoughts will keep you safe and add much to your enjoyment of a voyage: Think simple, think strong, think upside down.

(See Basic requirements)

SINGLEHANDERS

■ **If you're singlehanding, sleeping is illegal**

Rule 5 of the International Regulations for Preventing Collisions at Sea is exactly the same as Rule 5 of the United States Inland Navigation Rules. It states:

"Every vessel shall at all times maintain a proper look-out by sight and hearing, as well as by all available means appropriate in the prevailing circumstances and conditions, so as to make a full appraisal of the situation and of the risk of collision."

That's pretty explicit. But when a singlehander sleeps there is no look-out at all, proper or improper. It's an undeniable transgression of the rules.

So why aren't singlehanders charged and prosecuted? Why are organizations such as the Vendée Globe allowed to promote single-handed non-stop races around the world, where 20 or more yachts are blundering along at high speed (often maintaining an average of 14 knots or more) with no one keeping a look-out while their sole occupants sleep?

One possible answer is that in a collision with a ship, the yacht will come off worse. It's not necessarily true, and it doesn't take account of collisions between yachts. But why else would illegal sin-glehanding be condoned?

TIP: To cut down on the chances of collision, some singlehanders train themselves to wake up every 10 or 20 minutes and take a quick look around.

(See Singlehanding)

SINGLEHANDING

■ **How large a boat can you singlehand?**

A better way of asking that question is: How small a boat can you get away with? If you're young, fit, and uncomplaining, you can sail around the world in a 20-footer. But if you're more like the rest of us, you'll want to upsize a little, for more room and comfort down below.

Where does the upsizing end? It depends on so many individual requirements that it's impossible to set a physical limit or boat size that suits everybody, but there are two handy rules of thumb to consider here. The first is that a good big boat is more seaworthy than a good small boat. The second is that you should never singlehand a boat that's too big for you.

And just what is "too big?" Well, two factors come into play now: Can you raise, strike, and reef the mainsail in *all* conditions? And can you drop and (more importantly) weigh the anchor under all conditions? If you are comfortable about your abilities in these two respects, you shouldn't have any problems with the physical handling of the boat.

TIP: Size is not the most important quality of seaworthiness, so the best advice is to go as small and simple as you dare. Usually, that means something between 25 feet and 35 feet.

(See Singlehanders)

SLIP FEES

■ **Big boats get a better deal in port**

Port charges on ships are nearly always assessed on tonnage, which is actually interior volume or cargo-carrying capacity. But for some unfathomable reason, docking charges for yachts are assessed on overall length.

Now, we all know that a small increase in overall length will produce a surprisingly large increase in interior volume. Imagine the shape of a boat to be a cube, or part of one. If you double the size of that cube, you increase the interior volume by 8 times. According to prominent New York naval architect Dave Gerr, a 55–footer is actually 21 times bigger than a 20-footer, assuming similar proportions for each. Its taxable value is also 21 times greater.

But does a 55-footer pay 21 times the mooring fees? Not on your life. Nothing like it. Marinas normally charge by the foot. So if the fees are reasonable for 55-footers, owners of boats of 20, 30, and 40 feet are being robbed blind. And the smaller your boat, the more you're suffering.

If you think this smacks of the rich getting richer while the poor get poorer, you're right. Shame on marina operators. This is discrimination. It's time they were taken to task.

TIP: The bigger your boat, the less you'll pay in moorage, as a proportion of the boat's market value.

SOULS

■ Boats have souls and you can fall in love with them

It's rumored that the heads of sacrificial virgins were placed on the bows of newly launched ships in ancient times to appease the gods of the wind and the sea. When the head fell off, they believed the girl's soul had entered the ship.

Virgins aside, it's easy to believe that boats have souls. They often seem to have lives of their own. If you've ever paused to sneak glances at your boat dipping and lifting her head haughtily at anchor, you'll know what I mean. At sea, when she wriggles her stern over a passing swell, or disdainfully tosses aside a wave in a cloud of spray, it's even easier to believe.

Both men and women fall in love with boats. When a boat brings you safely through a storm, it's hard not to feel emotional attachment. And if you think about her in every quiet moment, it's a sure sign of romance.

As in other love affairs, there will be times when she will be ornery and expensive to keep. But at least she won't make eyes at other boats or run off to Las Vegas with them.

TIP: "The moment you begin to feel that a ship is a living thing, you are a sailor and her devoted slave." —A. H. Rasmussen.

(See Obsession)

SPEED

■ **There's always someone with a faster boat than yours**

One of the depressing facts of the sailing life is that no matter how fast your boat is, someone will have one that is faster. You may console yourself with the fact that big boats are naturally faster than small boats, but it's more difficult to accept defeat when a boat the same size as yours comes flying past.

Specially designed speedsters always pay a price, of course. They always sacrifice something: room down below, seaworthiness, durability, comfort, or reasonable price. But often—and mostly, in the case of the one-design classes—it's new sails that work the miracle.

I thought I was quite a hotshot in an 11-foot dinghy class until one light day when a rival boat came sneaking past with two grinning 250-pound men aboard. I ordered new sails immediately, and a few weeks later my petite wife and I won the national championships. New sails will do it. That's why some racing classes limit the number of new sails you can buy in a year. If you're tired of being passed, start talking to your sailmaker.

TIP: Fads, such as loose-footed mainsails, come and go because people suddenly find their boats sailing faster. But it's not the loose foot. It's the new material. A new regular main would do just as well.

(See Lies; Racing, Relative speeds)

SPINNAKERS

■ The most unseamanlike sail is a spinnaker

Sailing downwind was never a problem before we became addicted to the Bermuda rig. Squaresails, gaff mainsails, luggers, junks, and Arab dhows are all more suited to running before the wind than the tall triangle of the Bermuda sail shoved out to one side.

For better balance, the Bermuda rig needs a sail on the opposite side to the mainsail to even out the turning forces. Many racing boats are forced to use a parachute spinnaker, and cruisers are often tempted to follow their lead. But the spinnaker is a treacherous beast. Sir Francis Chichester, the famed British singlehander, called it "a lubberly sail." Richard Henderson, the American sailor and author, says it "can be a contrary devil to handle, and even fully crewed racing boats have had numerous problems with this temperamental sail."

Even the so-called cruising spinnaker or gennaker is suspect. It has no need for a pole, but sailmakers still had to work out a system to make it easier to set and strike. The sail is stuffed inside a long thin sausage skin of light fabric raised and lowered by its own built-in set of lines and blocks. Nothing's easy about spinnakers.

TIP: If you *have* to use a spinnaker, always keep the mainsail up so you can strike the spinnaker in its lee.

(See Sail materials)

SPLICING

■ Why go crazy trying to splice double-braid line?

For years I felt guilty about not being able to splice double-braid line. As one descended from a seafaring family, one who has always displayed prowess in the bosun's art, this failure to form a simple loop in the end of a rope has long been a secret blot on my escutcheon. But I've finally gotten over it. I no longer give a damn about eye splices in double-braid line. I'm no good at it and I don't care.

It's not as if I didn't try. Heavens, no. I have three different splicing tools and none of them did any good. I try now to forget the blighted hours I spent trying to shove those tools through, around, and under unyielding nylon and Dacron.

Master rigger Brion Toss describes the splice as "a bizarre, alien construction, and one that most people find intimidating." He got that right.

I make magnificent splices of all kinds in good old three-strand line. If I *have* to use double-braid line, I make my loops with bowline knots. Life's too short to splice double-braid.

TIP: Somebody told me the other day that the mistake I made was to use stiff old line. "You can only splice *brand-new* braid," he said. Too bad. It's too late now. I'm put off for life.

(See Running rigging)

STABILITY

■ Stable boats are stable upside down, too

Stability might be defined as the tendency of a vessel to return to an upright position. If it's a strong tendency, we say the boat's stable, or stiff. If it's weak we call her tender, or cranky. The trouble is that the forces acting to return her to an upright position vary with the angle of heel.

Some light boats with wide beam and shallow hulls appear to be very stable when they're upright. It's difficult to make them heel at all. But let a wave push them over to 90 degrees and they've hardly any stability left. A heavy, deep, narrow boat, on the other hand, might heel over quite easily for the first 15 degrees. She might feel quite unstable. But after 15 degrees she starts to stiffen up considerably. By the time she's over 90 degrees, her stability is at a maximum. Upside down, the beamy boat will be content to stay that way, whereas the narrow boat will immediately struggle to pull herself upright again.

Other factors affecting stability are draft, ballast, center of gravity, and hull shape.

TIP: A sailboat that starts out cranky but gains stiffness quickly as she heels will give a more comfortable ride at sea than an initially stiffer boat that reacts violently to every wave.

(See Capsize; Stability, tenderness)

STABILITY, TENDERNESS

■ When is a boat too tender for safety?

Most sailboats lacking in initial (or form) stability lose their tenderness as they heel and become reassuringly stiff. But if such a boat fails to start resisting heeling after she has reached an angle of 15 degrees or so, and continues simply to lie over and dip her gunwale in reasonably moderate winds, she's probably too tender for safety. If she won't stand up to all working canvas in 15 knots or so, don't hesitate: seek professional help, preferably from a naval architect.

Liveaboard cruising boats often lose stability imperceptibly as

their owners gather possessions over the years. This causes a boat's ballast keel to become an ever-smaller percentage of displacement.

The situation can be improved substantially by lowering weights wherever possible. These include internal ballast, water and fuel tanks, batteries, outboard engines clamped to the aft rail, life rafts, dinghies, provisions, and anything higher than the boat's center of buoyancy.

Keep your spars and rigging wire as light as possible. That goes for the sails and fittings, too. Hanked-on foresails improve stability more than roller-furling sails because they can be lowered in bad weather.

TIP: Lessen weight aloft. Because of the effect of leverage, every ounce off the top of the mast is worth a pound added to the keel.

(See Capsize; Stability)

STAINLESS STEEL

■ They lie—it's not stainless

One of the things boatowners learn very quickly is that a lot of stainless steel isn't stainless at all, no matter what the manufacturers claim. You just have to see those brown stains on the stanchions, the rigging wires, swim ladders, turnbuckles, and propeller shafts to know the truth of the matter. Those stains are a mild form of oxidation, or rust.

Stainless steel is a collective name for a group of alloys, some of which are more resistant than others to rusting. The best kind of stainless steel for boats is known as austenitic. It's very resistant to corrosion, thanks to its nickel content and higher levels of chromium. The two most common grades are 304 and 316. Type 316 is less bothered by corrosion than 304, but is not quite as strong.

Luckily, austenitic stainless steel is also less magnetic than other kinds, so you can use a small magnet to see if your stainless steel is of the highest grade. The more it's attracted to the magnet, the more likely it is to rust.

TIP: Stainless steel needs oxygen at its surface to form an anti-corrosive shield. If no oxygen is available, and it gets damp, it will rust as quickly as mild steel. That's why stainless-steel keel bolts are a bad idea.

STEERING

■ **You don't have to steer accurately at sea**

Inexperienced crews sailing offshore often feel the need to steer an exact compass course, particularly at night. That's not only very difficult but can lead to unhealthy feelings of guilt and stress. Long-term focusing on a dim compass bowl in a lively sea on a pitch-dark night is enough to drive you crazy.

An experienced sailor at the helm lets a boat's head swing to and fro as seems reasonable, mentally noting from the compass the range of her wandering. All the navigator needs from you at the end of your trick at the helm is an *average* course and speed. From that, the dead reckoning can be worked up in a trice.

Of course, if you're racing you'll want to steer the most advantageous course. That takes much more concentration, especially to windward at night when you have to sail by the seat of your pants to avoid stalling or falling off. An hour of that is enough for anybody. But then, ocean racing is for super-sailors; and best left to them, in my experience.

TIP: Write down the requested average course so it's visible from the helm. It's all too easy to forget what the navigator asked for. Wax pencil figures on a white cockpit bulkhead will prevent errors.

STORM TACTICS

■ Your keel shape dictates your storm tactics

When there's talk about keel shape you'll hear the expressions "long" or "traditional" keel, and "fin" keel. A long keel describes one that is long fore and aft, not a deep keel. A fin keel describes one that is short fore and aft but deep, shaped more like an airplane wing.

In general terms, long keels are found mostly on dedicated cruising boats and fin keels on racing boats or racers-cum-coastal-cruisers. Boats with long keels are better at looking after themselves in storms at sea. They're able to drift under bare poles with the helm lashed to leeward while the exhausted crew rests below.

Boats with fin keels usually fare better in heavy weather if they're kept moving by a larger, fresher crew. The small area of the keel is thus better able to dissipate the overturning energy of the waves into a greater area of water. Some fin-keelers will lie at an advantageous angle of about 50 degrees to the waves under a storm jib only, others will need to run before the wind.

TIP: Running before a storm requires a strong waterproof cockpit with large drains and solid hatch boards or doors, and safety harnesses with strong attachment points to prevent your being swept overboard if a wave boards from aft.

(See Trysails)

SURVEYORS

■ These experts don't *have* to pass any exams

Buying a used boat is a stressful business, especially for new sailors. The standard advice is to have the boat professionally surveyed because a few hundred dollars spent on a survey can save you many thousands of dollars if you buy a pig in a poke. It may even save your life.

But how do you find a good surveyor? There are no nationally recognized standards. Anyone can claim to be a surveyor. No qualifications are needed.

So how do you tell who's competent and who's not?

The Society of Accredited Marine Surveyors conducts its own internal exams for members, and the National Association of Marine Surveyors requires its members to maintain certain standards, so there is a valuable level of competence here.

Some marine insurance companies keep lists of recommended surveyors. Yacht brokers will give you recommendations, but there may be some self-interest involved. Boating associations, such as BoatU.S., and yacht mortgage companies will also usually give you an unbiased recommendation.

Most good surveyors have backgrounds in the marine trades. That includes boatbuilders, yacht architects, boatyard managers, and marine engineers.

TIP: It's best if the expert you consult is a sailor as well. Any surveyor who has experienced a storm at sea in a small sailboat is sure to do a very thorough survey.

T

TEAK AND VARNISH

■ **Don't varnish until you're ready to sell**

One of the problems with fiberglass yachts is that they can look a little sterile and insipid, like overgrown Clorox bottles. To compensate, designers often specify wooden details on deck to add a little warmth and traditional feeling. That wood is usually teak, which looks quite splendid when it's newly oiled or varnished.

But it doesn't stay splendid for long unless you commit yourself to a routine of regular maintenance. Most sailors grumble mightily about having to varnish when they should be sailing. The fact is, though, that teak can be left without varnish or oil and it won't be harmed. It's a naturally oily wood that resists rot. It eventually weathers to a silvery gray color—certainly not as attractive as the dark honey glow of varnished teak, but quite acceptable to most people.

TIP: Anyone planning to go long-term ocean voyaging might want to consider giving their teak six or seven coats of varnish and then a couple of coats of buff-colored paint on top. The paint protects the varnish and wood from ultra-violet degradation and will last for many years without maintenance. When the time eventually comes to sell the boat, strip off the paint and touch up the varnish underneath. Nicely varnished teak can add thousands of dollars to the resale price.

(See Maintenance, teak)

TENDERS

■ Inflatable dinghies aren't all that good

Most long-term cruisers end up with hard dinghies of wood, fiberglass, or aluminum even if they started out, as many do, with inflatables.

There are at least two good reasons for this:

- Inflatables suffer more damage from rough landing spots and exposure to the sun; and

- Inflatables are infinitely more attractive to thieves, particularly in third-world countries.

You'll find that traditional hard dinghies row and tow more easily, and are drier under way. If you ever have to send out an extra anchor in a choppy harbor, and your outboard is on the fritz, you'll be very glad you have a hard dinghy. Rowing an inflatable is never fun; in bad weather it can be near impossible to make headway.

When you're out cruising, your dinghy is the equivalent of the hard-working family car. In the planning stages of a voyage, most people don't realize just how many knocks it's going to take. If you can't repair a hard dinghy yourself, you'll find help available almost anywhere in the world. Major repair facilities for an inflatable, however, are few, far between, and comparatively expensive.

TIP: If you don't have space for a hard dinghy on deck, consider one of the many space-saving nesting designs made of two parts that fit inside each other and bolt together.

(See Dinghies)

TIDES

■ If you sail, you'd better know about tides

Let's say there's a nice steady breeze and you're making 6 knots through the water. If a 3-knot current is flowing against you, you'll make only 3 knots toward your destination. If that 3-knot current is flowing with you, you'll make 9 knots toward your destination. If you're not impressed by the difference between 3 knots and 9 knots (or three times the speed), you should be.

Tidal currents vary tremendously from place to place and time to time, so, if you sail, you badly need to know what the current is doing to you. You can get that information from annual tide and current tables for your area, either in book form or from the Internet.

It's no good trying to guess. Looking over the side or spitting in the water isn't going to tell you which way the current is going, or how fast. But a GPS receiver will indicate your speed and direction *over the ground*. By the simplest arithmetic you can compare this with your speed through the water, either taken from your regular speed indicator or estimated by shrewd guess, to find the speed of the current.

TIP: Work the tides. Anchor until the worst is over, or work the close-shore reaches where counter-currents and back-eddies often prevail.

(See Currents)

TOWING

■ If you're towed too fast, you'll probably sink

Be very careful when you accept a tow. Funny things can happen, especially if your displacement boat is towed too fast, which is only too likely to happen if a powerboat comes to your aid.

As a towed sailboat gathers speed, she digs herself a deep hole in the water. At her maximum hull speed (1.34 times the square root of the waterline in feet, remember?) she fits almost exactly in the hollow between two wave crests. Any faster than that, however, and she will be dragged willy-nilly up the back of the forward wave, allowing her stern to drop until water flows over the transom and floods the cockpit.

Here are two golden rules. First, make the towboat captain promise he won't exceed your hull speed. Second, just in case he does, arrange the towline so you can cast it off from your helm position. Don't ever be caught in a position where you can't abandon the tow immediately without problems.

Try to arrange a good communication system between the boats before you start off. VHF radios or walkie-talkies are a good idea, failing which manual systems or flashlight signals at night will have to suffice.

TIP: A nylon hawser or anchor line makes a good towline. If you have a centerboard, keep it in the stowed (fully up) position.

TRADE WINDS

■ **The clever way to roll down to Rio**

Running dead downwind for thousands of miles in the warm trade winds sounds like idyllic armchair sailing, until you try it. The trouble is that the armchair rolls continually from side to side and does its best to hurl you out.

Many sailors trying a trade-wind passage for the first time simply use their coastal rig of mainsail and large boomed-out foresail on the opposite side. They soon find out that this is an open invitation to the swells to rock them from gunwale to gunwale with the regularity of a metronome. Steering is tricky because the boat keeps wanting to round up, sail chafe is rampant, and the motion is vile.

Experienced voyagers usually concoct a special downwind rig of twin foresails. If they're flown forward in a deep V, they take a lot of the sting out of the rolling and, importantly, they ease the steering. If the sheets are taken to the tiller, you can even get the boat to self-steer.

TIP: Not many voyagers can bring themselves to do it, but you can cruise far more comfortably by tacking downwind in the trades instead of running dead downwind. It adds about 6 percent to the distance, but if it gives you more speed you won't lose any time.

(See Downwind sailing)

TRYSAILS

■ The sail you need for the worst of storms

There's a lot of confusion about the purpose of a trysail. Many sailors, even quite experienced voyagers, will tell you that you don't need an old-fashioned trysail because modern Dacron or Terylene sails are very strong. So, they contend, all you need is a third reef in your mainsail, rather than a trysail.

Well, they're missing the point. One of the trysail's most important jobs is to keep the bow pointed up toward the waves in very heavy weather, so that the boat rides in the safest position about 50 degrees off the wind. The trysail accomplishes this by carrying much of its area a long way aft, so the stern is forced away from the wind. As you reef a mainsail, though, exactly the opposite happens. The sail's center of effort creeps forward, allowing the bows to fall off the wind. Unless you're intentionally trying to lie ahull with no sail, that's not a good position to be in.

A proper trysail is shaped somewhat like a jib on edge and its clew (the pointy end aft) is made fast to fittings (or passed through blocks) on the boat's quarters.

TIP: For quick and easy setting, many circumnavigators keep a trysail permanently attached to its own track and bagged at the base of the mainmast.

(See Storm tactics)

U-V

UNLUCKY NAMES

■ Some names can bring you bad luck

Whether you're superstitious or not, you might want to consider whether the name of your boat is appropriate. And by "appropriate" I mean: is it likely to offend any of the gods of the wind and the sea? Presuming they exist, of course.

You may think it's nuts to be concerned about this most unlikely set of circumstances. You may also be surprised by the number of sailors who take the old superstitions of the sea very seriously. Many of us still regard the sea and its manifest mysteries with primal awe. We figure we need all the luck we can get. We don't wish to offend deities such as Aeolus and Neptune who were worshipped by our ancestors for thousands of years.

So we don't give our boats presumptuous names that invite retribution in the form of "bad luck." There are no *Storm Tamers, Wave Masters* or *Tsunami Blasters* among us. We don't pretend to be in charge of the wind or sea. We practice humility. Just in case.

TIP: It's also presumptuous to paint your hull green or blue, the colors of the sea. In old legend, boats had their own souls and could not presume to be part of the sea itself. White, the color of a spent wave, is permitted.

(See Luck; Renaming a boat)

UPGRADING

■ Even a brand new boat needs upgrading

It undoubtedly comes as a shock to many new owners to discover that they need to spend a lot more money on their brand-new production boats to bring them in line with their requirements. The fact is that boatbuilders work in a very competitive world and they naturally try to keep purchase prices as low as possible. So your new boat may come with regular winches instead of the self-tailers you lust after, and it may lack a dodger and an anchor windlass.

There are many expensive extras on most skippers' lists, including a better propeller, bigger anchor, extra sails, integrated electronics, radar, extra fuel and water tanks, an efficient heater, and so forth.

You should know that if you buy a new boat in the 35-foot range with the intention of doing extended cruising, the extra equipment you need can cost you as much as 25 percent of the purchase price.

TIP: Given the opportunity, it may be a better idea to buy a fairly new boat that has just returned from foreign voyaging or extended cruising at home. It will not only be less expensive to buy but it will also have all the essential extra gear a cruising boat needs, and with any luck it will all be working still.

(See Basic requirements; Yachting gear)

VENTILATION

■ Never shut your boat up tight

The healthiest boats have a minor gale of wind blowing through their interiors all the time they're at moorings or in marina slips.

You might logically assume that a boat shut up good and tight against the elements will stay nice and clean and dry down below but that's not so. Insects such as cockroaches will love you for it. Molds and mildews will show their appreciation by reproducing in vast, happy numbers and eating your upholstery. You'll soon have a boat that smells as foul as it looks.

Good ventilation was always a priority for preventing rot in wooden boats and it's just as important in today's plastic hulls. An adequate flow of air constantly drawn inside ensures that the cabin and its contents will be the same temperature as the outside air. That prevents the heavy freshwater condensation that occurs when warmer air inside comes into contact with surfaces cooled down by contact with the outside.

TIP: Several Dorade boxes with large cowls are needed for good through-flow, together with louvers in the companionway drop-boards. Remember that a 4-inch cowl moves almost twice as much air as a 3-inch cowl. Those little flat ventilators, with or without solar-powered fans, don't move much air, but are better than nothing.

(See Mildew)

VOICES FROM THE SEA

■ You'll wonder who's calling for help

Michael Stadler once wrote a book of great interest to sailors, called *Psychology of Sailing*. Stadler, a professor of experimental psychology at Bremen University, Germany, is a sailor himself. His book explained something that had puzzled me for many years— voices from the sea.

Anyone who has stood a lone night watch at sea has heard them. Sometimes a voice seems to be murmuring somewhere on deck. Sometimes there's a chilling cry for help coming from a passing swell. That's alarming. Boats have been known to turn back in a state of turmoil to search fruitlessly for a phantom person overboard.

Stadler explains that the noise of the wind and water in stormy weather contains all the frequencies that constitute speech or music. "It thus often happens that the sailor who has been exposed to this white noise for a long time, and who is also worn out from struggling against the storm, will succumb to the illusion that he is hearing voices or music."

TIP: It's nothing to get concerned about, says Stadler. You're not hallucinating or going mad. It's an entirely normal occurrence resulting from the brain's ability to filter out background noise and select frequencies of greater significance for human survival, such as those in the range of speech.

(See Hallucinations; Voices from the sea)

VOYAGING

■ Here's the vital difference between voyaging and cruising

Beginning sailors will hear a lot of oblique references to cruising boats and bluewater (or voyaging) boats. No one could blame them for being confused. Even among the experts there is little consensus about correct usage.

The essential difference is that the term cruising is much more loosely defined than the term voyaging. For example, you can go cruising for a week in the San Juan Islands of the Pacific Northwest, pulling into a sheltered anchorage or marina every night, and never sailing for more than four or five hours a day. Or you can cruise from Atlantic City to Fort Lauderdale, galloping down the Intracoastal Waterway or going "outside" and battling the Gulf Stream, or a combination of both. On the other hand, you can go cruising indefinitely and end up in the South Pacific or even rounding Cape Horn on the way to Sweden. So whenever you use the term cruising, you really have an obligation to add a narrower definition.

But when you go voyaging there's no fooling around with day-sails. You're crossing oceans. This is big-time stuff. The ultimate cruising. Voyagers dine at the very top of the cruising food chain.

TIP: You can tell voyagers from cruisers by what's hanging over their sterns. Cruisers have dainty barbecues. Voyagers have hefty self-steering windvanes.

W

WATCHKEEPING

■ Be sure to send your crew to bed on time

If you're doing ocean voyaging, coastal sailing, or any passage-making that involves a trip of more than 18 hours or so, you'll usually have to order your crew to go down below for some rest.

Many crewmembers, particularly the inexperienced ones, will resist. They won't want to miss out on the scenery or the warm sunshine. They'll want to be on deck where all the action is taking place. They'll say they can't sleep in the daytime. They may even be afraid they'll be seasick if they go below.

But an experienced skipper sets watches and makes sure his crew sticks to them. Crews who lack sleep and become exhausted are a liability if bad weather suddenly strikes. They make bad de-cisions and their reactions slow down.

There are admittedly many occasions when you can't sleep properly at sea, but even in gales most people find that simply

lying down on a bunk for several hours, dozing occasionally, provides the rest their bodies need to recuperate.

TIP: If you're afraid to spend your off-watch below because you might get seasick, take precautionary medicine before leaving port. Remember, too, that most people feel better when they lie down and close their eyes. Sitting is said to be the position that most encourages seasickness.

WATER

■ Here's how little fresh water you really need

If you've ever spent some time in the desert you'll be aware that most town-dwellers are profligate users of water. It's a tendency we have to learn to overcome very quickly when we put to sea because sailboats can't carry much fresh water. It's simply too bulky and too heavy.

For as long as I can remember, experts on public health have urged us to drink at least eight glasses of water a day, but I can assure you from personal experience that when you go cruising you can get by on far less, even in tropical climates. In *The Captain's Guide to Liferaft Survival* Michael Cargal says that you can last indefinitely on a pint a day in temperate climates, two pints in the tropics.

My family and I once averaged just under half a gallon a day each on a six-month voyage in a 31-footer, and that included water for cooking and bathing, though I should add that we bathed in salt water and then used a small garden spray filled with fresh water to wash off the salt.

TIP: For planning purposes, it's wise to count on a minimum of one gallon per person per day at a speed (for most medium-sized yachts) of 100 miles a day.

(See Drinking seawater; Freshwater supplies; Plankton)

WATERTIGHT BULKHEADS

■ **An inconvenient way to keep your boat afloat**

There are several ways to ensure that a sailboat won't sink. You can pack it with low-density material, or air bags, that will float it even if it fills with water. You can leave off the heavy keel, add another hull, build everything of wood, and have a non-sinkable multihull. Or you can chop your monohull up into separate spaces with watertight bulkheads that will prevent water from flooding the whole boat if one section is damaged.

Flotation material for ballasted hulls is very bulky. For example, to keep an average 35-foot fiberglass boat afloat you'd need about 160 cubic feet of foam—the equivalent of nine 18-cubic-foot kitchen fridges. That doesn't leave much space down below for anything else.

Bulkheads make more sense, and are mandated for some long-distance racers whose rules stipulate a minimum of three watertight bulkheads dividing the hull into four approximately equal compartments. They also have to have smaller collision bulkheads fore and aft.

As you can imagine, they are greatly inconvenient, especially when each internal access hatch has to be opened and shut behind you as you move through the hull. But they will keep you afloat.

TIP: You may need less internal flotation if you have a rubber dinghy or life raft you could inflate down below in an emergency.

WAVE HEIGHTS

■ **Why wave height is always exaggerated**

Small-boat sailors almost always overestimate the size of waves, not because they're natural liars but because of a little-known natural phenomenon. Briefly stated, it means that "down" isn't always where we think it is.

William Froude, a British naval architect, discovered in 1861 that no matter where your boat might be situated on the face of a large swell (no matter even if the bow is pointed to the sky) straight down to you will always be at right angles to the water's surface.

When you look aft in a following gale, your false "down" will fool you into believing that a near-vertical face of water is approaching. It then comes as a surprise when it seems suddenly to flatten out and pass underneath the hull without breaking.

This is easier to understand if you draw a picture of a boat halfway up the back of a large swell. Draw two lines, one at right angles to the surface and another, perpendicular to that one, representing your "horizontal" sightline to the approaching swell aft.

TIP: The only time you can judge the height of waves with any accuracy is when you are in the middle of the valley between two crests. Only at that fleeting moment will you be free of the illusion discovered by Froude.

(See Freak waves)

WEATHER HELM

■ The shameful thing nobody likes to admit

There is something in common between a woman who knowingly marries an imperfect man and a sailor who knowingly buys a boat with bad weather helm. Both are under the impression that they can change things for the better. Both are likely to be disappointed.

Owners of yachts suffering from weather helm are a tight-lipped lot when it comes to discussing their boat's fault, though they'll participate quite happily in any critical review of someone else's problem.

Weather helm is the amount of rudder needed to counter the

boat's tendency to round up into the wind. Anything greater than 4 degrees slows down your progress and generally makes for heavy, unpleasant work at the tiller.

There are many causes of weather helm, most of them interrelated, and there are several things you can do to lessen it, including adding a bowsprit or moving the mast forward, but most skippers resign themselves to suffering in silence.

It's almost impossible to know at the design stage whether a hull will suffer from excessive weather helm, so those sweet boats that lack it are usually the result of pure luck on the naval architect's part.

TIP: A boat with bad weather helm should be reefed early and sailed as flat as possible.

(See Balanced helm)

WHO'S IN CHARGE?

■ A sailboat is not a democracy

People around here have gotten quite spoiled by democracy. Women no longer have to chain themselves to railings in order to vote for their political leaders. Kids no longer have to be silent at the dinner table. They're allowed to speak now, for goodness' sake, without even having been spoken to first. And modern guests on yachts, well, they seem to think they have the right to sit anywhere they like, talk without permission, and even use the head without asking. Such extraordinary liberties.

There can be only one boss on a sailboat. By the very nature of things, a skipper must be a dictator—a benevolent dictator if you're lucky. There can be no democratic committee meeting about whether or not to take in a reef in the face of an approaching line squall, no split vote about whether to put the engine in reverse with the dock fast approaching.

Call me Captain Bligh if you must. I don't mind. Bligh, in fact, was a skilled navigator who applied the rules fairly and safely delivered those who only spoke when spoken to.

TIP: One of the persistent fantasies of democracy is to imagine you can be the boss and everybody's friend at the same time. Forget it. Just be the boss.

(See Responsibility)

WIND AT MAST HEIGHT

■ **The wind changes speed with elevation**

Life would be a lot easier for sailors if air were colored instead of being invisible. A smoky pink might be nice, or a cheerful yellow. Then we could see what was happening to our sails, and easily adjust them for maximum efficiency.

As things are, however, we have to do a lot of guessing. We also have to put great faith in the pronouncements of scientists who assure us that the moving air we call wind changes speed as it gets higher. Apparently, friction between the air and the ground, or water, slows down the lower layers of wind. The difference is perceptible, they tell us, even over the short distance from deck to masthead.

That in turn affects the murky business we know as apparent wind, a combination of the true wind and the forward movement of the boat. On the mainsail, it means that the apparent wind is freer at the head than the foot by about 5 or 8 degrees. That's why the head of the sail should fall off, with a gradual twist all the way up the leech.

TIP: Don't try to make adjustments. Your sailmaker will have built in the correct twist for most conditions.

WIND STRENGTH

■ Double the speed is quadruple the force

There's something very interesting about wind. If it doubles its speed, it strikes the sails with four times the force. I've never understood why. It doesn't seem very logical to me. I believe it has something to do with twice the number of molecules combining with twice the amount of energy, but I guess I wasn't concentrating when that came up in science class.

In any case, it explains why a wind of 30 knots generates a pressure of 3.6 pounds per square foot on a sail, while a wind of 60 knots, just double that speed, generates a pressure of a tad above 14 pounds per square foot.

It also explains why the need to reef often seems to arise very suddenly. Most medium-sized cruising sailboats have to reef when the wind is blowing 16 to 18 knots—but that's only twice the speed of an 8-knot breeze that hardly makes the boat heel at all. It seems extraordinary that a mere extra 8 or 10 knots in windspeed can make the difference between a quiet jog and a gung-ho ride with gunwales awash. But it does.

TIP: You'll recognize the truth of this formula when you're under way and change from a run to a beat. The difference in wind force is quite amazing.

(See Reefing)

WINDLASS

■ Don't expect miracles of your anchor windlass

The manufacturers of anchor windlasses warn people not to expect too much from them, but that doesn't stop many sailors from abusing them. Windlasses are designed to lift only the weight of the anchor and its line. They aren't meant to drag a heavy cruising boat up to her buried anchor in choppy seas against a strong current or heavy wind. But it happens all the time.

The makers try to salvage their reputations by advising sailors to choose much bigger windlasses than they really need, so they won't wreck the machinery before the warranty runs out. Nevertheless, the windlass slaughter continues.

Do your pocketbook a favor by taking the strain off your anchor rode. Sail or power up to the anchor and simply let the windlass take up the slack. If you do this, you can get away with a much smaller and less expensive windlass; and if you have nothing more than a manual windlass, your arms and back will be very grateful.

TIP: To relieve your windlass of much unfair strain, fit a chain stopper to the foredeck or the bow roller. It's a simple pawl that clinks into a link of chain and jams it when the chain tries to run backward out of the roller.

(See Anchoring)

WOMEN SAILORS

■ **Women sail as well as men; maybe better**

It took 80 years for a woman sailor to equal Joshua Slocum's achievement of sailing around the world singlehanded in 1898. Krystyna Chojnowska-Liskiewicz, of Poland, was the first woman to do it, in 1978, and she was followed closely in the same year by Dame Naomi James, a New Zealand-born Briton who was the first woman to circumnavigate solo via Cape Horn.

Women have been making significant solo voyages since Englishwoman Ann Davison became the first female to cross the Atlantic alone in her 23-footer, FELICITY ANN, in 1953, but their numbers have been quite low, compared with men. Perhaps they have more sense.

But whatever prevented them from competing in quantity, it never affected their quality. They've demonstrated that they have the guts, the talent, the physical strength, and the will to do anything a man can.

In fact, on February 8, 2005, a Englishwoman called Ellen MacArthur became the fastest person ever to sail around the world non-stop and alone. Dame Ellen took 71 days, 14 hours, in the 75-foot trimaran *B&Q*.

TIP: Never underestimate a woman on land or on sea. Remember Queen Boadicea, the greatest of British heroines, who led her warriors into battle against the might of the Roman Empire in AD 61-63, and won. And think of Ellen MacArthur.

WOODEN BOATS

■ Wood is still the best material for boatbuilding

If you've ever dreamed of building your own boat and sailing away to the South Pacific you'll already know something that most modern sailors don't: for a one-off hull, nothing beats wood.

You *can* build a custom hull out of metal, fiberglass, or concrete, but wood has advantages over all of them if it's treated in the modern way by sealing it with epoxy resin and sheathing it with fiberglass.

Wood is Nature's gift to sailors, a miracle material in many ways. It's lighter than fiberglass, aluminum, steel, and concrete of the same strength—and it floats. It's easy to fashion and clean to work with. The ease with which it accepts fastenings is a joy to amateur boatbuilders and when you wreck your boat, wood is biodegradable.

Wood is a natural insulator that will keep your cabin warm in winter and cool in summer. Laminated with resorcinol glues and flooded with thin epoxy, it forms a monocoque construction of great strength. It's flexible and impervious to borers. And, best of all, it's very satisfying to the human soul.

TIP: If you seal the wood with epoxy and protect it with a layer or two of fiberglass over the outside, the lifespan of your boat should equal that of a solid fiberglass hull.

(See Building a boat)

WRITING ABOUT SAILING

■ Don't expect to make a living from books or articles

Don't sail away with the idea that you can write articles and books to pay for your round-the-world trip. Lin Pardey, one of the best known modern cruising authors, once told me she reckoned you'd need six or seven books in print before you could live off the proceeds.

If you write a book that sells for $15 you'll likely get publisher's royalties of about 10 percent. A boating best seller in the USA is generally taken to be one that sells 10,000 copies or more. So the most a new author is likely to make, over a number of years, is $15,000. And remember, the field is very crowded with would-be authors willing to accept less than you, just to get their names in print.

Magazine articles are a total crapshoot. I have sent articles to two of the largest sailing magazines in the country and waited more than a year for a reply. The payment magazines offer for an article of 2,000 words with pictures varies from $100 to $1,000, depending on the publication's prestige, circulation, and bankroll.

TIP: Marketable skills more likely to produce a cruising income are the ability to repair diesel engines, fridges, watermakers, SSB and satellite radios, computers, and electronic instruments, together with general yacht repairs, deliveries, sailmaking, varnishing, and—says cruiser Don Casey—cutting hair.

Y-Z

YACHT CLUBS

■ **Not all yacht clubs are snobbish**

There seems to be a general perception among landlubbers that yacht clubs are hallowed halls filled with snooty snobs in tailored jackets and gold-braided caps. I guess there are a handful of clubs like that in America but the vast majority don't deserve that reputation any more than the average boater deserves to be called rich.

My present club, for example, doesn't even own a clubhouse. We gather once a month for a potluck meal in a pleasant waterfront hall that we rent for the occasion from the local port authority. We listen to the reports of the various committees, we tell each other tall tales about our sailing exploits, and we generally have a good time with nary a tailored jacket to be seen.

The first club I belonged to was much the same, except that it had a great clubhouse on the waterfront. It was run by no-nonsense soldiers just returned from World War II who wanted a place to build and store racing dinghies. Oh, and a pub in which to talk things over after the race.

TIP: Most yacht clubs are friendly toward beginners. They know the best diesel mechanics and the cheapest boatyards. They organize races that hone your sailing skills and dinner dances that hone your social skills.

YACHT DEFINITION

■ **So what is a yacht, anyway?**

What defines a yacht? When can you boast to prospective dates that you own a yacht rather than an overgrown sailing dinghy? It's not at all clear, unfortunately.

Dictionaries tell us that the Dutch word *jacht* from which yacht derives, means to hunt, or chase. *Jachtschip* was the name given to small, fast, maneuverable sailboats that chased and intercepted other vessels, for whatever reason.

But the dictionaries don't set size limits for yachts. Their definitions are so broad as to include sailboards and jet skis. Even the venerable *Chapman Piloting* falls into that trap with its very concise definition: "A yacht is a power or sail vessel used for recreation and pleasure, as opposed to work."

No size limit at either end, you note. By my reckoning a yacht ought to be a pleasure vessel that is at least partially decked, have some accommodations (at least a couple of bunks), and a length of at least 20 feet. Nothing less is going to impress most dates.

TIP: There might not be much point in trying to define the word yacht any longer. It's gradually falling out of favor, as is the word yachtsman. We're more likely now to refer to ourselves as boaters who own sailboats or powerboats—with yacht-like looks and accommodations, of course.

YACHTING GEAR

■ **Everything made specially for yachts is more expensive**

Some retailers deliberately raise their prices for what they perceive to be rich boating customers. I have been in a hardware store belonging to a large national chain where the identical 3M masking tape cost 10 percent more in the boating aisles than it did in the household paint section a few feet away. People tell the same story about paint, paint stripper, stainless-steel bolts, and many other items.

But that's not the real reason why yachting gear costs so much. Price-gouging aside, there are two good reasons why it's more expensive. Firstly, it mostly needs to be of higher quality, since everything on a boat works in the most atrocious conditions of high humidity, salt-laden air, galvanic action, ultra-violet rays, rain, and often snow and ice.

I'd feel much happier about trusting my life to the quality-tested shackle that's pulling me up the mast than I would the cheap knock-off from the Far East.

Secondly, the boating market is a comparatively small one in which marine manufacturers don't gain the same benefits of high-quantity production that others enjoy.

TIP: When it comes to masking tape and paint stripper, buy cheap if you must. But when it has to do with safety or longevity, buy only the best yachting quality. Grin and bear it.

(See Upgrading)

ZINC BLOCKS

■ **Small sacrifices save expensive fittings**

A process called galvanic corrosion will gradually eat away expensive pieces of underwater hardware on your boat unless you do something about it. Electronic bugs will nibble away day and night at your expensive bronze propeller, your rudder fittings, your through-hull fittings and any other pieces of metal that live underwater.

This process can be controlled by offering something tastier for the bugs to bite on. That something is zinc.

If you connect a piece of zinc to a piece of bronze underwater, it forms an electric cell in which the least noble metal corrodes and the more noble metal survives.

A list known as the galvanic series tells you which metals are most noble, or passive, and which are least noble, or active. Aluminum and zinc are the least noble and are most likely to deteriorate through galvanic action. Copper, bronze, nickel, and stainless steel are among the most noble, and therefore most resistant to being eaten away.

Brass, an alloy of zinc and copper, will react rapidly underwater until only weak, spongy copper remains. Never use it on the exterior of a boat.

TIP: Sacrificial zinc blocks must preferably be fastened directly to the metal they are to protect. If that's impossible, a good electrical connection via copper wire is permissible.

(See Electrolysis)

Appendix

Some Useful Tables and Formulas I Wish I'd Known About

Note: Some of the material in this appendix has already been touched upon briefly in the body of the book. It is repeated here in more convenient, tabulated form.

■ Formulas

Areas
Circle: Multiply radius x radius x 3.1416
Cylinder: Circumference x height. Add areas of circles at ends
Parallelogram: Base times vertical height
Sphere: Multiply diameter x diameter x 3.1416
Triangle: Half length of base x vertical height

Volumes
Cone: Radius x radius x height x 3.1416. Divide answer by 3
Cube: Length of base x side x side
Pyramid: Side at bottom x height. Divide answer by 3
Sphere: Diameter x diameter x diameter x 0.5236

■ Conversion factors

Horsepower to kilowatts: multiply horsepower by 0.7457
Kilowatts to horsepower: multiply kilowatts by 1.341
Knots to miles an hour: multiply knots by 1.152
Miles an hour to knots: multiply miles by 0.868

■ Other useful rules and formulas

Alternator size

If you have a modern multi-step regulator, your alternator should be capable of putting out (in amps) between 25 and 40 percent of the total number of amp-hours in all your batteries.

If you don't have this superior regulation, you should limit alternator output in amps to 10 percent of your battery bank's total amp-hours. That will give your batteries the longest life, but it will obviously take much longer to charge them fully.

(See Battery needs)

Anchor sizes

These are reasonable minimum sizes for average wind strengths in sheltered waters and good holding ground:

Plow anchors—1 pound of anchor weight for every foot of boat length.
Bruce and similar anchors—85 percent of corresponding plow anchor's weight.
Danforth and similar anchors—55 percent of corresponding plow anchor's weight.
Fisherman (traditional) anchors such as the Herreshoff and Luke—150 percent of corresponding plow anchor's weight.

Anchor line, minimum length

Small boats can anchor in shallower water than big boats, so the minimum length of anchor rodes varies. A good plan is to allow a minimum of 6 feet of rode for every foot of your boat's length. (Remember, the word "rode" includes chain *and* nylon line if any.) If you regularly anchor in deep water (40 feet or more) you'll need a minimum rode of 240 feet.

Anchor line scope

The anchor scope is the ratio between the depth of the water, *measured from deck level to the sea bed*, and the length of the anchor line. Most anchors won't grip the bottom unless you give them a scope of at least 3 to 1, that is, you let out line equal to three times the depth of the water. For average conditions, a scope of 4 to 1 or 5 to 1 is better. In storm conditions, a scope of 7 to 1 is recommended if you have enough swinging room.

Anchor rode sizes

The best anchor rode for a cruising boat is all-chain. If that makes too much weight in the bows, use a rode of three-stand nylon with a length of chain, equal to the length of the boat at least, attached to the anchor. As a rough rule, the nylon should be about twice the diameter of the chain. Measure the chain as if you were measuring rod: that is, across a single piece of the metal rod forming the links. Don't measure across the whole width of a link.

Boat length	Nylon diameter	Chain diameter
Up to 25 feet	$7/16$ inch	$3/16$ inch
26 to 30 feet	$1/2$ inch	$1/4$ inch
31 to 40 feet	$9/16$ inch	$5/16$ inch
41 to 45 feet	$5/8$ inch	$3/8$ inch
46 to 50 feet	$3/4$ inch	$3/8$ inch

Arm and hand angles

There are many times when it's handy to be able to estimate quickly a vertical or horizontal angle. You already have the tools at your fingertips. When you hold one arm out straight, these are the approximate angles you're looking at:

20 degrees: Widely spread hand, from thumb tip to fingertip.
15 degrees: Fingers formed into tight fist, thumb extended.
10 degrees: The width of your fist alone.

5 degrees: From one side of your fist to middle knuckle.

3 degrees: The width of your thumb alone.

2 degrees: The width of your little finger.

Barometer readings

In the middle latitudes (30 degrees to 60 degrees north and south) the average barometer reading at sea level is 1,013 millibars, or 29.90 inches.

A high barometer (fair weather) reads 1,033 millibars, or 30.50 inches. A low barometer (foul weather) reads 999 millibars, or 29.50 inches.

Very dangerous storms, called weather bombs, are indicated by a barometer falling at least 1 millibar an hour for 24 hours in a row.

Battery needs

To estimate the size of battery or batteries you need, simply make a list of all the electric equipment on your boat and estimate how many watt-hours each piece uses daily. For example, a tape deck drawing 15 watts, and used, on average, for 4 hours a day, rates 60 watt-hours.

Add up all the daily watt-hours and divide them by the voltage in your electrical circuit. (That will be 12 volts in most cases, maybe 24 or more on bigger boats.) The answer will be in amp-hours. Batteries are rated according to their storage capacity in amp-hours, so you can readily make a choice. Except for one important thing.

Normal batteries found on boats offer you only 40 percent of their amp-hour capacity for normal use. That's because it isn't healthy for the battery to be discharged more than 50 percent of its capacity, even if it's a deep-cycle battery, and also because it's not usually practical to top up the last 10 percent of capacity with ordinary charging. Thus, you can't regularly withdraw 60 percent of the amp-hours stored in your battery bank. Consequently, you'll have to increase the amp-hour capacity you calculated that you need. You'll have to multiply it by 2.5.

For example, if you found your needs were 100 amp-hours a day, you'd have to provide batteries totaling 250 amp-hours, 40 percent of which is 100 amp-hours.

(See Alternator size)

Berth lengths
Try all the berths before you buy a boat. Some production boats have bunks that are too short for an adult. For comfort, berths should be at least 6 feet 4 inches long and 1 foot 9 inches wide. Since we're not all six-footers, one berth in four may be only 6 feet 1 inch long.

Block sizes
The sheaves of blocks used with fiber lines should have a diameter not less than eight times the rope diameter. For long life and easy rendering, wire-rope sheaves should ideally have a diameter at least 40 times the wire's diameter. They mostly don't, however, and that shortens the life of the wire.

Capsize screening formula
The resistance a sailboat offers to being capsized can be measured with the aid of the U.S. Sailing Association's capsize screen formula. It is an indication of a boat's *initial* stability, that is, her stiffness or resistance to being heeled over. It is not an indication of a boat's *ultimate* stability, which is her resistance to remaining completely upside down after having been capsized by a large wave.

To determine the capsize screening formula, divide your boat's displacement in pounds by 64.

Find the cube root of that number.

Take the beam in feet and tenths of a foot, and divide it by the cube root you just worked out.

If the answer is less than 2, your boat is considered relatively safe from capsizing in rough water.

Be aware, however, that even the largest yachts can be turned turtle by a breaking wave with a height equal to 55 percent of their length on deck.

Course errors

It's sometimes difficult to maintain a compass course in bad weather or choppy seas. And sometimes it's easy to make a slight mistake when you're plotting a bearing on a chart. Navigation is an imperfect science on a small boat, but have you ever wondered about the practical effect of a few degrees of error in steering or plotting?

Here's an indication: if your steering is wrong by 5 degrees, you'll end up one mile off course for every 11.5 miles you run.

Cruising cost

Just as people on land spend varying amounts of money on everyday living, so do sailors who go long-term cruising. You can spend as much as you care to on a yacht and its maintenance, according to the style and luxury you seek, but what is of more interest here, perhaps, is how little you can get away with if you weren't born with a silver spoon in your mouth.

It probably should come as no surprise that if you are frugal on land, you're likely to be frugal on a boat, too. Two of the world's most experienced cruisers, Lin and Larry Pardey, figure the cost of cruising this way:

Take all your everyday onshore expenses. Subtract all your costs for cars or trucks. Subtract two-thirds of your expenses for your rent, your mortgage, your mooring costs, and your clothing. Add 33⅓ percent to the cost of your food.

The result, say the Pardeys, is pretty close to what you'll spend when you go long-term cruising.

Denaming ceremony

Have you noticed what silly names other people give their boats? As the buyer of a used boat, it's only natural that you (a civilized, intelligent, educated person of wit and charm) would want to change the old name to something more suitable. But you're scared, right? You've heard that it's unlucky to change a boat's name.

Well, not if you take precautions. One of the most popular articles I ever wrote was Vigor's Interdenominational Denaming Ceremony. It described the steps I took when I wanted to rename a 31-foot sloop I intended to sail from the Indian Ocean to the United States with my wife and 17-year-old son.

It consisted of a formal little denaming ceremony, a request to the ancient gods of the wind and the sea to erase the boat's name from their records, and to accord her the same protection she had enjoyed from them before, when she was re-baptized under a new name. It worked for me, and I've had no complaints from the hundreds of people who have used it since.

You will find a free printable copy of the ceremony and full instructions if you do an Internet search using the words "denaming ceremony." Alternatively, you can go to <www.48north.com> and look in the article archives.

Dinghies, carrying capacity
The U.S. Coast Guard has a formula to determine how many people a dinghy (a boat under 20 feet) can safely carry in *calm* weather:

> Number of people = overall length x beam in feet ÷ by 15.
> For example, a 12-foot dinghy has a beam of 4.5 feet.
> 12 x 4.5 = 54. Divide 54 by 15 = 3.6. Round up to 4 people.

The average weight of a person is usually taken to be 160 pounds for purposes of this formula.

If the weather isn't calm, think carefully about how many people your dinghy should be carrying.

Displacement-to-length ratio

Knowing the relationship a boat's displacement bears to her waterline length gives you some interesting insights into her handling and capabilities.

For boats of equal weight, the one with the longer waterline is known as a light-displacement craft. She'll be faster, livelier, trickier to handle, and more uncomfortable at sea. She's likely to have a shallow hull with a fin keel and a detached rudder.

The one with the shorter waterline, a heavy-displacement boat, will be slower, easier on her crew and gear, and usually more resistant to capsize. She'll likely have a more full-bodied hull with a longer keel (horizontally) and a rudder attached to the hull or a skeg.

Racing boats are mostly of light displacement and cruising boats of heavy displacement.

The displacement-to-length ratio is the waterline length divided by 100. Cube the result and divide it into the boat's displacement in tons.

Here's how the numbers stack up:

Very heavy displacement—380 or more
Heavy displacement—320 to 380
Medium displacement—250 to 320
Light displacement—120 to 250
Very light displacement—50 to 120
Ultralight displacement—50 or less

Dock lines, length and size

In addition to your normal dock lines, carry at least two that are a quarter longer than your boat. These are for use as springs, which prevent movement fore and aft. You'll find them invaluable in areas where you have to tie up alongside a fixed pier or jetty when the tides have a large range.

As for the size of dock lines, a good rule is to allow a minimum of ⅛ inch of line diameter for every 9 feet of boat length. In other words, a 36 footer should carry lines at least ½ inch in diameter (36 ÷ 9 = 4 x ⅛ = ½).

Engine fuel consumption
A very useful rule of thumb is that a diesel engine needs roughly 1 gallon of fuel per hour for every 18 horsepower you're *using*. In other words, if you're running a 36-hp engine at half speed, you can expect to use about a gallon for every hour of running. If you're running at full speed, you'll use 2 gallons an hour.

Four-stroke inboard gasoline engines need quite a lot more fuel. They consume about 1 gallon per hour for every 10 horsepower *used*. Gasoline outboard engines mostly are even less fuel efficient, and two-stroke engines devour more than four-strokes.

To calculate your fuel reserves, count on using one-third of your supply to reach your destination, one-third to get back, and one-third for an emergency reserve.

Engine life expectancy
Almost all new cruising boats are fitted with diesel auxiliary engines these days. Most of them weren't specifically designed for boats but are adaptations of tractor engines or light industrial engines. They prefer a dry cool workspace and they like to work quite hard for long periods at a time. On yachts, they mostly work for short periods in appalling conditions, squeezed into hot, airless little compartments with bilge water floating inches beneath them.

So, while a diesel engine on land will usually run for at least 8,000 hours without a major overhaul, the average marine diesel aboard an auxiliary sailboat gets 5,000 hours.

And while gasoline engines in cars run for an average of nearly 3,000 hours before needing an overhaul at 100,000 miles, the one in your sailboat will probably only run for 1,500 hours before needing attention.

Incidentally, if you use your boat only on weekends and for short vacations, you're likely to log only 200 engine hours a year. In theory, that translates to 7 or 8 years of trouble-free running for a gasoline engine and 25 years for a diesel. In practice, the atrocious working conditions, salt air, and neglect will almost certainly shorten these times according to the level of abuse the engine must endure.

Engine size

You can't push a displacement sailboat at anything much above its hull speed, no matter how much horsepower you install. So the biggest auxiliary engine that makes sense is one that will give you hull speed plus a little extra power to compensate for headwinds and choppy waves.

The needs of most cruising boats are filled by an auxiliary engine that produces 4 horsepower per long ton of displacement. So a sailboat displacing 10,000 pounds would get along just fine with an 18-horsepower engine. (10,000 pounds ÷ 2,240 = 4.46 tons x 4 = 17.84 hp)

This size engine may sound surprisingly weak-kneed in an age when many automobile engines produce 250 horsepower but, believe me, it's sufficient. Don't be tempted to increase it by much.

(See Hull speed)

Fenders

Carry a minimum of four fenders and preferably six. They should be at least 1 inch in diameter for every 5 feet of boat length.

Flooding speed

Most bilge pumps cannot cope with the inflow of water from a reasonably sized hole in the hull. Your priority should be to try to stem the flow somehow, either by stuffing cushions or something similar in the hole from inside, or by covering the hole with a collision mat or sail from the outside. That should slow down the flow enough to enable your pumps to cope while you make more permanent repairs. But unless conditions are ideal, a surprisingly small hole will sink you in short order.

For the record, here's the formula for rate of flooding from an underwater hole:

Incoming gallons per minute = D x square root of H x 20
(D = the diameter of the hole in inches and H = height in feet to which the water must rise to reach outside water level—in other words, the depth of the hole *below* water level.)

Note that a mere 2-inch-diameter hole 3 feet below the waterline will let in 69 gallons a minute, or more than 4,000 gallons an hour. A high-capacity power pump is rated at 3,000 gallons per hour.

Galvanic series

The galvanic series doesn't sound very exciting, unless you are a proton or an electron, but it's of vital importance to boaters. It's an indication of what metal on your boat is likely to eat some other metal, perhaps a bit that's keeping the vessel afloat.

Galvanic corrosion begins when two metals far apart in the galvanic series are connected underwater by a conductor. They form a rudimentary electric cell, in which electrolytic corrosion eats away the less "noble" metal. The process even takes place out of water, between, for example, the aluminum in a mast and the stainless-steel screws holding a fitting in place.

Metals close together in the galvanic series have little or no reaction with each other, but the farther apart they are, the more vigorous the corrosion. A copper nail that falls into the seawater bilge of an aluminum boat will eventually eat a hole right through it, as the less noble metal, aluminum, corrodes away.

Here is a shortened version of the galvanic series, showing the metals most used on boats. It starts with the least noble metals, the ones that will be sacrificed, and ends with the most noble metals, which will be spared:

Magnesium
Zinc
Aluminum
Mild steel
Stainless steel (active)
Lead
Tin
Brass
Copper
Bronze
Monel
Nickel
Stainless steel (passive)

Note that stainless steel will corrode almost as fast as mild steel in its active state, when it is in still water with no access to oxygen. But when it has a ready supply of oxygen from air or water, it is passive.

Hull speed

A displacement hull is one that pushes water down and around itself as it makes progress, as opposed to a planing hull that skims along on top with much of its body clear of the water.

Displacement hulls at full speed fit into a large, self-made wave that has its crests at the bow and stern. Now, the speed of a wave is 1.34 times the square root of its length between crests. Thus, the maximum speed of a displacement hull is often said to be the same as that of the wave it creates.

For example, you'll often hear that a sailboat with a 25-foot waterline will have a maximum speed of 6.7 knots (square root of 25 = 5 x 1.34 = 6.7). But that's not quite true because a boat can sometimes exceed the speed of the wave it's trapped in, at least for brief periods. What is true is that the hull-speed formula tells you the maximum speed that your boat can reach *reasonably easily.*

Any attempt to go faster and push a displacement boat up the back of the wave she's sitting in requires an extraordinary extra amount of power and a very flat run aft to provide dynamic lift.

On the other hand, the speed of a planing hull is governed almost exclusively by the power-to-weight ratio. If you can keep total weight down to 40 pounds for every 1 horsepower available, you'll do 25 knots or so. And if you can keep the weight down to 10 pounds per horsepower, you'll do 50 knots.

Knots and their weakness

Most of the line we use aboard sailboats is much stronger than it needs to be simply because thinner line is harder to handle, but you should at least know that if you are stressing a line to its limits, a knot will weaken it considerably. And permanently.

Any fiber line that has been stressed to its working load or more with a tight kink in it, such as a knot, should be regarded as having lost about a third of its ultimate strength.

Different knots also have different effects. Here's how some common knots react:

Knot	Strength reduction
Anchor bend	24 percent
Bowline	40 percent
Clove hitch	40 percent
Reef knot	55 percent
Round turn and two half hitches	35 percent
Sheet bend	45 percent

Miles, statute and nautical

On the Great Lakes and major rivers of the United States, as well as the Intracoastal Waterway, measurements are given in statute miles of 5,280 feet each. Elsewhere, the nautical mile rules. It has now been established at 6,076 feet, and is roughly ⅐th longer than the statute mile. To convert nautical miles to statute miles, multiply nautical miles by 1.15. To convert statute to nautical, multiply statute by 0.875.

Navigation lights, visibility

The navigation lights of a sailboat are notoriously difficult for other vessels to see. They're not very bright and are often obscured by sails or spray. Always try to fit the biggest lights you have power for.

Here's how far you can see white lights working from a 12-volt system through *clear* glass or plastic when conditions are perfect:

A 10-watt bulb is visible for about 2 miles.
A 24-watt bulb is visible for about 3 miles.

When it comes to red and green lights, the range is far less:

A 10-watt bulb is visible at little over 1 mile.
A 24-watt bulb is visible for about 2 miles.

Phonetic alphabet

To sound like a professional when they ask you to spell your boat's name, copy this list and place it near your Victor Hotel Foxtrot radio:

Alpha	November
Bravo	Oscar
Charlie	Papa
Delta	Quebec
Echo	Romeo
Foxtrot	Sierra
Golf	Tango
Hotel	Uniform
India	Victor
Juliet	Whiskey
Kilo	X-Ray
Lima	Yankee
Mike	Zulu

Propellers, walking sideways
Because the bottom of a propeller works in slightly denser water than the top, the prop tends to walk sideways through the water like a wheel on an axle. The effect is usually far more pronounced in astern gear than ahead. Thus, a right-handed propeller (one that turns clockwise in forward gear, viewed from astern) will tend to thrust the stern to starboard in ahead gear, and to port in reverse. Use this knowledge to your advantage by approaching a dock port-side-to and engaging reverse gear to tuck your stern in.

Ropes and stretch
Sometimes we need stretch in a line and sometimes not. Nylon is the rope that stretches to absorb shocks and then returns to its original length. It's the ideal line for anchor rodes and dock lines. Polyester, known by the trade name Dacron, doesn't stretch like nylon, and is used on cruising boats for halyards and sheets.

Nylon stretches about 14 percent at 30 percent of its breaking load, but regular Dacron stretches only 5 percent. Special Dacrons such as Sta Set-X are even more resistant to stretching, averaging only about 3.24 percent, which is excellent for halyards that you don't want to have to adjust too often.

There are more exotic fibers used on racing boats that stretch even less. Spectra gets stretch down to 1.25 percent, for example, and Spectra XLS-900, at 0.95 percent, stretches even less than wire rope.

Rudder stall angle
Be careful with rudder movements. If you put the rudder over too far it will stall and have hardly any steering effect at all. A free-standing spade rudder will stall when the blade is angled at about 20 degrees to the flow of water. After that, its major effect is to slow you down. As soon as the boat starts to turn, however, you can put the rudder over a little more, to a maximum of about 35 degrees.

Rudders that are attached to the hull or a skeg are more forgiving. They don't stall as quickly as spade rudders, but they don't react as quickly either.

Sail materials

The two materials most used for sails on cruising sailboats are Dacron and nylon. Dacron is used for all fore-and-aft sails; nylon is used for spinnakers and light-weather foresails.

Racing yachts and high-tech cruisers often use laminated sails with sandwiches of Kevlar, Mylar, and Spectra but the lives of such sails are generally shorter and they are more expensive to start with.

Sealant types

Sealants and bedding materials come in a wide array of confusing choices. Read the fine print and experiment at your leisure. Meanwhile, here are some suggestions that will keep you out of trouble:

- Polyurethane sealant is also a strong glue. Use it for permanent joints only. Don't use it to bed fittings you might want to remove later. Don't use it with plastics such as Lexan or ABS. Most polyurethanes cannot be painted—check the instructions.
- Polysulphide is available in single and double packs. The twin packs cure more quickly. Use it for all kinds of sealing and bedding except plastics, which it will melt. It remains pliant and is not as strong an adhesive as polyurethane. You can paint or varnish over it.
- Silicone is a good bedding and gasket material that is safe with all materials, including plastics. Most silicones lack the aggressive adhesive qualities of polyurethane but there are new hybrids with improved adhesion that could be difficult to remove if necessary. Once again, read the labels. Silicone will stick nicely to almost anything dry but you can't paint or varnish over it.

Size of boat for singlehanding
Supersailors take 60-footers around the world non-stop and singlehanded but most of us are neither supersailors nor want to be.
So, how big a boat can a reasonably fit person manage alone, with
safety? There are two major factors that come into play for anyone
intending to do a long cruise.

- Can you easily control the largest sail on board? Can you
  safely lower it, smother it, and get gaskets around it?
- Can you raise the anchor by hand if the winch breaks down?
  Age obviously comes into play here. An old rule of thumb is
  that a person of reasonable strength and fitness can raise a 60-
  pound anchor and chain without any mechanical aids. But as
  you get older, you might well find a 35-pound CQR as much
  as you can cope with on a regular basis.

There are many suitable seaworthy boats between 25 feet and 40
feet that are considered splendid singlehanders. The big difference
is in price, accommodations, and speed.

Solar charging rates
The amount of electricity generated by a solar panel depends on
many things, of course, including the size of the panel, the materials used, the strength and amount of sunlight available, and the
angle that the panel presents to the sun.
But from these many variables we can extract a useful rough
rule:

If you take the rated wattage of a rigid solar panel, you can expect to collect about one-quarter of that number in amp-hours
every day.

In other words, a 35-watt panel will supply your 12-volt battery
with 8.75 amp-hours (35 ÷ 4) per day. That probably sounds low

to you, but it's realistic. You could probably double the output by adjusting the panel so that it's square to the sun's rays all day long.

Tacking angles

Most top-notch racing boats in calm water can sail within 40 degrees of the true wind. Most cruising boats are happy if they can get within 50 degrees, that is, a difference of 100 degrees on the compass before and after tacking.

In choppy seas and headwinds almost all boats will need to fall off the wind by 5 degrees or more to gain enough power to drive through the opposing waves.

Just for comparison, and to make you feel better, here's what other sailing vessels could manage:

Viking longboats and square-riggers: 70 degrees.

Clipper ships: 65 degrees.

Tides

The tide rises and falls about half its height in the middle third of its time range. In other words, a tide flooding for six hours will rise half of its total range in the middle two hours.

In the first hour of the new tide it rises $\frac{1}{12}$; in the second hour, $\frac{2}{12}$; and in the third hour, $\frac{3}{12}$ of the total height. It tapers off in reverse order: $\frac{3}{12}$ in the fourth hour, $\frac{2}{12}$ in the fifth hour, and $\frac{1}{12}$ in the sixth hour. Just remember 1,2,3,3,2,1 to get an idea of the height of the tide over the chart datum at any time.

Books I Wish Someone Had Told Me to Read

Here's a mere handful of the hundreds of books covering almost every boating subject imaginable. But if you read all of these, I can assure you that you'll be better informed and safer than 90 percent of amateur boaters.

Some are out of print now, but they're often available from booksellers or Internet sources such as <www.abebooks.com> or <www.alibris.com>.

Boat design

—Brewer, Ted. *Understanding Boat Design.* Camden ME: International Marine, 1994.

Clean, easily digested narrative for beginners by one of North America's most respected naval architects.

—Skene, Norman L. *Elements of Yacht Design.* Dobbs Ferry NY: Sheridan House, 2001.

A classic for anyone interested in the process of creating a yacht, or for anyone who wants to know how design changes performance.

Circumnavigating

—Slocum, Joshua. *Sailing Alone Around the World*. Dobbs Ferry NY; Sheridan House 1995.

An enthralling tale by the first person to sail around the world alone. Written with modesty and humor that belies his profound skill.

—Hiscock, Eric. *Around the World in Wanderer III*. Oxford: Oxford University Press, 1956.

The author and his wife Susan rank among the all-time cruising greats, not only for their expertise as mariners, but also for the quality of their writing and photography.

Cruising

—Chiles, Webb. *The Open Boat: Across the Pacific*. New York: W. W. Norton, 1982.

Chiles sailed almost all the way around the world alone in an open 18-foot Drascombe Lugger. This books describes his 7,000-mile voyage from San Diego to the New Hebrides.

—Bardiaux, Marcel. *The Four Winds of Adventure*. Adlard Coles: London, 1961.

Another extraordinary adventurer but little known in the English-speaking world. His exploits in his 30-foot homemade boat eclipse those of Moitessier, Captain Bligh, and even Shackleton.

Engines

—Calder, Nigel. *Marine Diesel Engines: Maintenance, Trouble shooting, and Repair*. Camden ME: International Marine 2001.

Calder, a sailboat cruiser himself, gained his extensive knowledge and became an international authority the hard way, by repairing diesels on boats.

—Sherman, Edwin R. *Outboard Engines: Maintenance, Troubleshooting and Repair*. Camden ME: International Marine, 1997.

The author covers the basic operating principles of two-stroke and four-stroke outboard engines with clear explanations and diagrams.

Knots

—Ashley, Clifford W. *The Ashley Book of Knots*. New York: Doubleday, reissue of 1944 edition.

The mother and father of all knot books features 3,900 knots and 7,000 illustrations. It's far more than you need but makes a wonderful present if you can persuade someone near and dear to buy it for you.

—Toss, Brion. *Chapman's Nautical Guides: Knots*. New York: Hearst Marine Books, 1990.

Toss, a professional rigger, is passionate about knots and this book shows it. He appeared on public television stations as "Mr. Knot."

Literature

—Jonathan Raban, editor. *The Oxford Book of the Sea*. New York: Oxford University Press, 1992.

For anyone interested in boats, this is entrancing stuff, more than 500 pages of extracts from the finest, most evocative writing about the sea and small craft from AD 900 to the present day.

Maintenance

—Casey, Don. *This Old Boat*. Camden, ME: Intermational Marine, 1991.

Casey, the author of a wide range of boating books, combines lucid writing here with decades of hands-on experience. It's a much-lauded book that provides all the knowledge you need to care for, or completely rebuild, any fiberglass boat.

Meteorology

—Watts, Alan. *Instant Weather Forecasting*, 2nd. ed. Dobbs Ferry NY: Sheridan House, 2001.

A tried and tested favorite carried aboard by many renowned voyagers. It features 24 color pictures of common cloud types and tells you what kind of weather they foreshadow.

Navigation

—Larkin, Frank J. *Coastal Navigation Using GPS*. Dobbs Ferry NY: Sheridan House, 2003.

Odds are that you'll now be using GPS in waters where the hand bearing compass and dividers used to rule, so this book pragmatically melds the old techniques of coastal navigation and pilotage with the new.

—Blewitt, Mary. *Celestial Navigation for Yachtsmen*, 2nd ed. Camden ME: International Marine, 1994.

Probably the most famous book about sextant navigation in small boats. Tautly written, simple to understand, nothing other than addition and subtraction involved. It's been going strong for over 40 years.

Racing

—Linskey, Tom. *Race Winning Strategies*. Dobbs Ferry NY: Sheridan House 1995.

Patterned on Linskey's colorful character Deep Dakron and his series in *Sail* magazine, this book is as entertaining as it is informative. Good sound advice from a well-informed author.

Rigging

—Toss, Brion. *The Complete Rigger's Apprentice*. Camden ME: International Marine, 1997.

Toss is an unconventional but conservative author, although not always the easiest to understand. Nevertheless, this book is shot through with useful hints and facts unavailable elsewhere.

Rules of Thumb

—Vigor, John. *The Practical Mariner's Book of Knowledge.* Camden ME: International Marine 1994.

Yes, shameless self-promotion, I know, but these 420 rules of thumb, tested by mariners over the centuries, will keep you out of trouble under almost all circumstances.

Sails

—Ross, Wallace. *Sail Power: The Complete Guide to Sails and Sail Handling.* New York: Alfred E. Knopf, 1975.

This book is still the bible for serious racers and cruisers. While some of the technical theory is now out of date, the practical, well-illustrated information is superb. Out of print but widely available used.

Storm survival

—Coles, K. Adlard. *Heavy Weather Sailing*, 4th ed. Camden ME: International Marine, 1992.

Yachting World magazine called this book "A really important work . . . brilliant and authoritative." *Ensign* described it as "Undoubtedly the most authoritative and complete book on the subject available." What more can I say, except that I agree with every word?

Other books of interest

READY FOR SEA!
by Tor Pinney

"...an easy read, packed with good advice. Even experienced cruisers will pick up a thing or two from this one."—*Latitudes & Attitudes*

"...presents clearly and concisely what it takes to provision a boat and sail it confidently..."—*SAIL*

HANDBOOK OF OFFSHORE CRUISING, 2nd Edition
The Dream and Reality of Modern Ocean Cruising
by Jim Howard

"…an immensely practical work. This encyclopedic volume has become a standard reference for bluewater sailors, particularly those planning extended cruising in mid-size sailing vessels."—Rodney Stevens, *Charleston Daily News*

MARINE ELECTRICAL & ELECTRONICS BIBLE
by John C. Payne

"Everything a sailor could possibly want to know about marine electronics is here...as a reference book on the subject it is outstanding."—*Classic Boat*

"...this is, perhaps, the most easy-to-follow electrical reference to date."—*Cruising World*

"All in all, this book makes an essential reference manual for both the uninitiated and the expert.—*Yachting Monthly*

THERE BE NO DRAGONS
How to Cross a Big Ocean in a Small Sailboat
by Reese Palley

"A delightful blend of information and stories, with emphasis on the human aspect of sailing. Witty, irreverent and inspirational with as much 'why to' as 'how to. '"—*Cruising World*

"…funny, raucous, insightful, anarchistic, entertaining, instructional; seamanship with a difference."—*WoodenBoat*

INSTANT WEATHER FORECASTING
by Alan Watts

"Gives the layman the magical art of weather forecasting..."—*Motor Boat*

"...a sure-fire bestseller..."—*The Yachtsman*

"...another gem that's a dog-eared favorite..."—*Coastal Cruising*

"...a popular forecasting guide since its first printing in 1968...particularly useful for the boating aficionado."—*Bulletin of the American Meteorological Society*

Sheridan House
America's Favorite Sailing Books
www.sheridanhouse.com

Other books of interest

A SPLENDID MADNESS
A Man • A Boat • A Love Story
by Thomas Froncek
"One of the most dangerous of all mid-life crises is the suddenly blooming love affair between a landlubber and a boat. In his instructive, sometimes very funny book, Tom Froncek tells how he not only survived but conquered many perils and surprises to make himself into a capable, happy sailor." John Rousmaniere, author of *Fastnet, Force 10* and *After the Storm*

CATBOAT SUMMERS
by John E. Conway
Chronicles a decade's worth of adventure in New England waters through a series of short tales, each recounting one of the Conways' many extraordinary experiences aboard their 100-year-old wooden catboat, BUCKRAMMER. From the hilariously ill-fated participation of a fleet of catboats in Boston Harbor's Sail 2000 Parade to a chilling, phantasmal encounter amidst fog and darkness and even a pilgrimage to the yard where BUCKRAMMER was born, readers will be enthralled by Conway's compelling narrative and whimsical humor.

FLIRTING WITH MERMAIDS
by John Kretschmer
"Not only has John Kretschmer lived a life wildly festooned with adventure, romance, and outrageous characters — his reality outstripping our most Walter Mittyesque sea fantasies — now he has gone and turned it all into a collection of yarns that incite yet more envy among those of us stuck behind landbound computers. Not only can the sailor sail — through hurricanes and civil wars — but the sailor can write. It's a hell of a read." —Fred Grimm, *Miami Herald*

SEASONED BY SALT
A Voyage in Search of the Caribbean
by Jerry Mashaw & Anne MacClintock
Mashaw and MacClintock are not your average sailors. Their story brims with humor and high adventure and reflects a deep respect for and understanding of the history, people, and economy of the many Caribbean islands that they visit. "...captures the feel of sailing among the Caribbean islands and realizing what matters in life."—Daniel Hays

Sheridan House
America's Favorite Sailing Books
www.sheridanhouse.com